GLOBETROTTER™

Travel

C000259733

JAMAICA

ROBIN GAULDIE

NEW
HOLLAND

NEW
HOLLAND

Fifth edition published in 2013
by New Holland Publishers (UK) Ltd
London • Cape Town • Sydney • Auckland
10 9 8 7 6 5 4 3 2 1

website: www.newhollandpublishers.com

Garfield House, 86 Edgware Road
London W2 2EA, United Kingdom

Wembley Square, First Floor, Solan Street
Gardens, Cape Town 8001 South Africa

Unit 1, 66 Gibbes Street
Chatswood NSW 2067, Australia

218 Lake Road
Northcote, Auckland, New Zealand

Distributed in the USA by
The Globe Pequot Press
Connecticut

ISBN 978 1 78009 162 4

This guidebook has been written by independent
authors and updaters. The information therein repre-
sents their impartial opinion, and neither they nor the
publishers accept payment in return for including in the
book or writing more favourable reviews of any of the
establishments. Whilst every effort has been made to
ensure that this guidebook is as accurate and up to date
as possible, please be aware that the facts quoted are
subject to change, particularly the price of food,
transport and accommodation. The Publisher accepts
no responsibility or liability for any loss, injury or
inconvenience incurred by readers or travellers
using this guide.

Publishing Manager: Thea Grobbelaar
DTP Cartographic Manager: Genené Hart
Editors: Thea Grobbelaar, Carla Zietsman,
Nicky Steenkamp, Tarryn Berry, Sean Fraser
Design and DTP: Nicole Bannister, Éloïse Moss
Cartographers: Genené Hart, Inga Ndibongo,
Tanja Spinola, Elaine Fick
Picture Researchers: Felicia Apollis, Shavonne
Govender, Colleen Abrahams, Rowena Curtis
Reproduction by Resolution, Cape Town
Printed and bound by Craft Print International,
Singapore.

Photographic Credits:
Danita Delimont Stock/awl-images.com: cover; **John
Burke:** 41; **Robin Gauldie:** 4, 21, 94, 97, 118; **Image
Select:** 14, 22, 30, 36; **Life File/Sue Davies:** 112,
115, 117; **Life File/Sean Finnigan:** 66, 69; **Life File/
Juliet Highet:** 73 (top), 92; **Life File/Emma Lee:** 12,
24; **Larry Luxner:** 35, **Jeanetta Baker/International
Photobank:** 6, 79; **Peter Baker/International
Photobank:** title page, pages 19, 20, 25, 62, 76, 81,
85, 90, 93; **Pictures Colour Library:** 29; **Richard
Sale:** 7, 9, 11, 13, 15, 16, 17, 18, 23, 26, 27, 33, 37,
39, 40, 42, 43, 44, 45, 48, 50, 51, 52, 53, 55, 56,
57, 58, 59, 65, 67, 70, 72, 73 (bottom), 84, 86, 87,
95, 98, 99, 102, 105, 106, 108, 109, 110; **Laurence
Wood:** 28, 116.

Keep us Current
Information in travel guides is apt to change, which
is why we regularly update our guides. We'd be
grateful to receive feedback if you've noted something we should include in our updates. If you have
new information, please share it with us by writing
to the Publishing Manager, Globetrotter, at the office
nearest to you (addresses on this page). The most
significant contribution to each new edition will
receive a free copy of the updated guide.

Cover: *Alligator Hole, Black River Town, Jamaica
South Coast.*
Title page: *Extensive white-sand beaches fringe the
Ocho Rios area, one of the most thriving resorts in
the Caribbean.*

CONTENTS

1
Introducing Jamaica

You know beyond a doubt when you have arrived in Jamaica. The weather is warmer, the insistent pulse of reggae music is on the air, and the cooling breeze from the Caribbean brings a whiff of poinsettia flowers, coconut oil, rum punch and a hint of ganja – the distilled aroma of a Jamaican holiday.

Jamaica is a rapidly developing country. The capital, **Kingston**, is a city of more than a million people, with all the urban potential of a fast-growing capital. Dotted around the island's shores are dozens of holiday **resorts**. Offering everything from barefoot simplicity to up-market sophistication or round-the-clock entertainment, they attract hundreds of thousands of visitors annually from Europe, North and South America and even Japan.

However, there is little overlap between urban Kingston and tourist Jamaica, and there are other aspects of Jamaican life that most visitors usually only get to glimpse from an air-conditioned minibus. In little villages in the hilly interior, rural folk work on sugar and coffee plantations or continue to scratch a living outside the cash economy from tiny patches of land.

In the mysterious, impenetrable jungle valleys of the **Cockpit Country**, the proud **Maroon** people maintain customs and a unique dialect closer in many ways to their West African ancestors than to the forward-looking young professionals of Kingston. Amazingly, some stretches of Jamaica's coast have not yet felt the full impact of tourism and primitive fishing canoes hollowed from a single tree trunk still stand in place of jet skis.

TOP ATTRACTIONS

*** **Negril:** lively but laid back, with the best beach, restaurants and nightlife.
*** **Montego Bay:** busiest resort, with good beaches and great shopping.
*** **Port Antonio:** peace and quiet amid gorgeous scenery.
** **Blue Mountain Peak:** finest view in Jamaica.
** **Rio Grande:** river rafting through giant bamboo forests.
** **YS Falls:** walk to the top, then plunge into the pools.
** **Black River:** Cruise through virgin forest and meet a crocodile.

◀ *Opposite: Colourful tour boats line the mouth of the Negril River.*

THE LAND

Jamaica is the biggest island in the English-speaking Caribbean and the third largest in the entire Caribbean region. It lies approximately 500 miles (800km) south of Miami, and its nearest neighbours are Cuba, less than 80 miles (130km) to the north, Haiti, about the same distance to the east, and the tiny Cayman Islands to the west. Shaped like a long, irregular oval, Jamaica is some 150 miles (240km) from east to west and 50 miles (80km) from north to south.

It is, in many respects, the embodiment of the Caribbean dream island. If your taste in holidays embraces sandy beaches, warm waters in a dozen tones of blue and turquoise, and a steady flow of delicious tropical cocktails, Jamaica approaches perfection.

However, there is much more to Jamaica. Behind every beach resort, hillsides cloaked in shades of tropical green beckon you to explore further this fascinating island. When Christopher Columbus came to Jamaica in 1493 he discovered a land of well-watered virgin forests, named by its indigenous Arawak people **Xaymaca** – 'the land of wood and water'. That name is still very apt today, despite five centuries of settlement and the introduction of sugar cane and coffee plantations, bauxite mines, and modern towns and resort complexes. Landing on a Jamaican beach today, Columbus would probably be astounded by the tourist development, but he would still be able to recognise the woods, rivers and waterfalls of his Jamaica.

Mountains and Rivers

Inland, much of the country is ruggedly mountainous. Jamaica is in fact a relatively high island, with almost half land at an altitude of over 1000ft (300m). In the east, not far from Kingston, Jamaica's highest summit rises from the **Blue Mountain** range to a height of 7402ft (2256m), while the **John Crow Mountains** continue further to the east. In the western part of the island the thickly wooded limestone hills of the **Cockpit Country**, with their curious karst rock formations – once dubbed 'The Land of Look Behind' – are still mostly trackless, to be explored only on foot.

Although it has many small streams, Jamaica has only a few proper rivers. The **Rio Grande**, rising in the Portland mountains, and the **Great River**, forming the boundary between St James and Hanover, are the largest – though neither more than 66ft (20m) at its widest. There are no natural or man-made lakes.

Seas and Shores

Kingston lies on the south coast, about 40 miles (64km) from the east end of the island and on a natural harbour. The capital is home to almost one in three Jamaicans, and is Jamaica's only big city. But it is the north coast which

▲ *Above: San San Bay's beautiful waters have made it an exclusive resort area.*
◄ *Opposite: The Great River is one of the largest watercourses in Jamaica.*

GREEN FLASH

No visitor who has been privileged to glimpse it will soon forget the green flash. This rare phenomenon of the Caribbean sky occurs just as the last sliver of sun sets below the horizon. If the sky is absolutely clear of cloud, dust and pollutants – an increasingly rare occurrence – light refraction through the atmosphere can cause a vivid emerald flash which can last for two seconds.

CLIMATE

At 18°N of the Equator, Jamaica has a **hot** and **humid** climate year round with almost no regional variation around the coast, though steady breezes on the **north coast** – the **Doctor Breeze** – make it more pleasant than **Kingston**, which swelters in a sheltered bowl of mountains with little relief from the heat. On the coast, temperatures average 28°C (82°F), with a maximum of 32°C (90°F) and a minimum of 27°C (80°F). On higher ground, around **Mandeville**, temperatures average around 6°C (11°F) less than on the coast. On the heights of the **Blue Mountains**, temperatures average 9°C (16°F) less than at sea level. July to October is hurricane season, and although hurricanes are far from an annual event, tropical storms and frequent downpours make the island somewhat less attractive to visitors during these months.

has traditionally seen the lion's share of Jamaica's tourism development. **Montego Bay** boasts Jamaica's second international airport and both 'Mo Bay' (Montego Bay) and **Ocho Rios**, midway along the north coast, are popular ports of call with US-based cruise ships. Beach resorts and villa complexes occupy almost every stretch of sandy beach between the two. **Port Antonio**, further east on the north coast, is another centre for more up-market tourism.

Jamaica's south coast sees far fewer tourists by comparison. An exception is Negril, on the extreme southwest corner of the island, which has rocketed from sleepy fishing village to full-scale international resort status in less than two decades, and is currently Jamaica's fastest-growing resort area.

Climate

While Jamaica's coast basks in tropical sunshine for much of the year, with little variation in temperature, settlements in the hilly hinterland enjoy cooler temperatures, especially at night.

By the sea, the temperature averages 28°C (82°F) year-round, rising as high as the low 30s at midday and falling into the mid-20s at night. Sunscreen is an essential; air conditioning is usually not. In the highlands around Mandeville, temperatures average around 21°C (70°F) year-round, while in the heights of the Blue Mountains, days – and especially nights – are much cooler than on the coast. Annual rainfall averages 78 inches (1980mm). It can rain heavily at any time of year, but the heaviest rainfall is between May and November. Naturally, this is the least popular time to visit the island, though many visitors from the UK and continental Europe come to Jamaica during these hot and humid months, to take advantage of the low off-season hotel prices. Most North American visitors, however, tend to come to Jamaica only during the winter months.

JAMAICA	J	F	M	A	M	J	J	A	S	O	N	D
AVERAGE TEMP. °C	30	30	30	32	32	33	33	33	33	32	32	32
AVERAGE TEMP. °F	86	86	86	90	90	92	92	92	92	90	90	90
RAINFALL mm	25	25	25	75	100	75	50	100	150	175	150	25
RAINFALL in.	1	1	1	3	4	3	2	4	6	7	6	1
DAYS OF RAINFALL	1	1	1	6	7	6	5	10	12	14	12	1

The south coast receives much less rain than the north, and the northeast – in the shadow of the Blue Mountains – is the wettest part of the island.

Like all Caribbean islands, Jamaica is occasionally hit by hurricanes and tropical storms. Hurricane Hugo struck in 1989, Ivan in 2004 and Tropical Storm Gustav in 2008, but three major hurricanes – Charley, Katrina and Wilma – all missed Jamaica between 2004 and 2006. Hurricanes and tropical storms are most likely to occur in July and August. The Jamaican proverb runs: 'June, too soon; July, stand by; August, you must; September remember; October, all over.'

Wildlife

Jamaica shares many plants and animals with other Caribbean islands and with the Americas, and there are also many species endemic to the islands. Unfortunately, some Jamaican bird and reptile populations have been reduced because of loss of habitat and predation by pests, which prey on eggs and fledglings. Nevertheless, Jamaica still has more than 250 **bird species**, 26 of which are indigenous. They range in size from the tiny **bee hummingbird** – the smallest of four species of hummingbird found in Jamaica – to giants like the **frigate bird**, an unmistakable predator with its long, hooked bill, forked tail, pointed wings and black plumage. Seen everywhere is the **'John Crow'**, a buzzard which circles high above the streets, hillsides and beaches alike. Another scavenger, the bright-eyed, glossy black **Antillean grackle**, will hop onto your table to steal scraps.

Reptiles indigenous to the island include the **Jamaican iguana** and the rare **American crocodile**, while **mammals** include the rabbit-like **coney** – a species of agouti – and the harmless vegetarian **manatee** sometimes spotted swimming in south coast bays and rivers.

▼ Below: Rare crocodiles are found at the Great Morass in St Elizabeth Parish.

Plant Life

Like its wildlife, Jamaica's plant life is a mixture of native and exotic. The **royal palm**, native to the island, is far outnumbered by the coconut variety, an import from the East Indies. Other native plants include the **pineapple**, **guava**, **soursop**, **pimento**, and the **lignum vitae** tree. More than 500 kinds of **fern** flourish in the steamy climate, as do **orchids** – more than 200 species – and **bromeliads**.

HISTORICAL CALENDAR

7th century AD–15th century AD: Jamaica settled first by Arawak then Caribbean people from South America.

1493 Christopher Columbus makes landfall at St Ann's Bay.

1510–1534 First Spanish settlements established and African slaves imported.

1655 British invasion force ousts Spaniards. Slaves left by the departing Spaniards escape into the uninhabited mountains, where they form the first Maroon settlements.

1658 Spaniards try to recover the island but are defeated at Battle of Rio Nuevo.

1660s Port Royal becomes a notorious haven for a buccaneer fleet under the British flag which harries Spanish fleets and colonies.

1670 Spain formally cedes Jamaica to Britain.

1690 First of several island-wide slave uprisings, led by Cudjoe. British troops and militia brutally crush the rebels and their Maroon allies in the first Maroon War.

1692 Earthquake destroys Port Royal.

1694 French fleet raids Jamaica but is beaten at Carlisle Bay.

1739 Maroon treaty gives the Maroons land and self government but obliges them to hunt out and return runaway slaves.

1760 Coromantee slave rebellion.

1795 Second Maroon War.

1807 Britain ends slave trade.

1831 Sam Sharpe's rebellion is brutally quelled.

1834 Britain abolishes slavery.

1865 Paul Bogle's rebellion is crushed and hundreds of rebels are executed.

1872 Kingston becomes seat of colonial government.

1907 More than 800 Jamaicans die in the great Kingston earthquake.

1938 Economic depression triggers riots and protests. The formation of People's National Party (PNP) by Norman Manley and first trade union organisation by Alexander Bustamante.

1944 Britain grants full self government to Jamaica.

1962 Jamaica becomes independent country within the British commonwealth. Sir Alexander Bustamante becomes first prime minister.

1972 PNP led by Michael Manley wins its first election.

1978 Bob Marley hosts concert to urge end to political violence.

1980 JLP (Jamaican Labour Party) led by Seaga wins election after a wave of pre-election violence in which several hundred people are killed.

1988 Hurricane Gilbert does great damage to homes, businesses and agriculture.

1989 PNP returns to power on new moderate left platform.

1992 Michael Manley retires as PNP leader and prime minister of Jamaica.

1993 Manley's successor PJ Patterson re-elected as prime minister.

2004 Jamaica affected by Hurricane Ivan.

2006 Prime Minister PJ Patterson resigns in favour of Portia Simpson Miller.

2007 JLP leader Bruce Golding elected prime minister. Jamaica hosts cricket World Cup. New Norman Manley International Airport opens in Kingston.

2010 Tropical Storm Nicole causes flash floods, deaths and extensive property damage.

2012 Jamaica celebrates 50th anniversary of independence.

HISTORY IN BRIEF

In a region of microstates where the population is more often measured in tens of thousands than in millions, Jamaica's size, energy, and a long line of bold and out-spoken leaders from every shade of the political and cultural spectrum have made it a pace-setter for many of its Caribbean neighbours.

Arawaks and Caribs

The earliest people to settle Jamaica were wiped out – along with their culture and language – by European settlers within two centuries of the arrival of the Spaniards, so we know little of them beyond what archaeological discoveries and the writings of the first Spanish navigators can tell us.

The placid **Arawaks**, who originated in what is now Venezuela, island-hopped through the Caribbean in their seagoing canoes over several centuries and seem to have arrived in Jamaica around AD650. Living on the sea and on abundant native fruit and vegetables, they settled around the coast but ignored the mountainous, impenetrable jungles of the interior. The Arawak idyll lasted for some 750 years until it was brutally interrupted by the warlike **Caribs**. Of similar Amerindian origin, the Caribs arrived in fleets of canoes to prey on Arawak villages, looting, enslaving and, on occasion, eating their less aggressive cousins. A similar pattern prevailed throughout much of what is now known as the Caribbean, named by the European invaders after these early aggressors. Fierce though the Caribs were, however, there was much worse in store for the native peoples. By the latter half of the 17th century, both the Arawaks and Caribs had disappeared, victims of slavery, disease and deliberate genocide.

The Spanish Main

Christopher Columbus made landfall off St Ann's in 1493, ushering in more than three centuries of colonisation, war, piracy and slavery.

◄ Left: An exhibit from the Arawak Museum near Spanish Town.

CARIBS

The fierce seafarers who gave the Caribbean its name originated, like the Arawak, in Central America, and fared through the Caribbean in giant canoes. But instead of settling peacefully, the Caribs ravaged the Arawaks, enslaving women and children and killing and eating the men. By Columbus's time, they had conquered the **Lesser Antilles** and were raiding Jamaica. Their ferocity failed to save them from the lethal impact of colonisation.

▼ Below: Columbus's landfall eventually led to the full mapping of Jamaica.

Despite all the evidence to the contrary, Columbus remained convinced that Jamaica and its neighbours lay close to the coast of China – the legendary Cathay – and its fabulous riches. Following in his wake, however, came a second wave of **Spanish** conquistadors, whose discoveries of Aztec and Inca gold in Mexico and Peru quickly put Jamaica in the shade. While the conquest of South America and its riches suddenly started to attract soldiers and settlers by the thousand, Jamaica became a backwater, valued only for the safe anchorages, fresh water and supplies it afforded Spanish vessels en route to more important Spanish colonies in the Americas. For approximately a century and a half, the Caribbean was known to Europe simply as the **Spanish Main**. Pirates and privateers – some of them under the flag of England, France or the Dutch Republic, others flying the Jolly Roger – regularly attacked Spain's treasure galleons, but Spain remained supreme until the 1660s.

Bonne: Map of the island of Jamaica 1778

The British Arrive

By the second half of the 17th century, Spain had been weakened by almost a century of wars with its European neighbours, and France, Britain and the Netherlands were all eyeing its lucrative Caribbean possessions.

In 1655, using the excuse of war with Spain in Europe, a **British** fleet sailed into what is now Kingston Harbour. With the British guns threatening their capital of Santiago de la Vega (today's **Spanish Town**) the Spanish garrison sailed off to the much stronger Spanish island colony of Cuba, leaving behind slaves whom they had freed and provided with weapons in the hope that they would fight a bush war against the British. Refusing to fight for their former masters, however, the freed slaves fled deep into the interior, where they set up little kingdoms. These **Maroons** (from the Spanish *cimarron*, meaning 'wild') were eventually to become a major problem for the British authorities, providing refuge for escaped slaves.

Some three years later, the Spanish troops returned and tried to drive the British out but were trounced at **Rio Nuevo**. Britain then set out to make life extremely uncomfortable for the Spanish colonies, raiding settlements and attacking supply fleets. Britain was not yet a world-class naval power, and throughout the 1660s the British government allowed privateers – pirates in all but name – to attack the Spaniards in the name of the Crown. In 1670 Spain formally surrendered Jamaica to England by signing the **Treaty of Madrid** and, despite an attempt by a **French** fleet under Admiral Jean du Casse to invade the island in 1694, Jamaica was to remain firmly in British hands for almost three centuries.

Buccaneers and Privateers

At first, British control of Jamaica was slack. Port Royal, the first British capital, which stood on the long spit of land sheltering Kingston Harbour quickly became a nest of pirates and was known as 'the wickedest city in the world'.

BUCCANEERS

The first buccaneers were a motley crew of **castaways** and **runaways** who lived by hunting wild boar and cattle, and curing meat – called *boucan* – to trade with passing ships for tools, powder and shot. They were known as *boucaniers* and when they formed an alliance, the **Brethren of the Coast**, to prey on Spanish shipping, the name became synonymous with piracy.

France and England hired them with 'letters of marque and reprisal' to attack enemy shipping. In the **Dutch War** of 1665 they saved Jamaica for England, and a grateful governor let them turn Port Royal into their headquarters – hence 'the wickedest city in the world'.

▼ Below: The tomb of Lewis Galdy, who survived the Port Royal earthquake.

At war at various times with the Netherlands, France and Spain, the British authorities turned a blind eye to the buccaneers of Port Royal – as long as they attacked only foreign shipping. Many of the pirates became extremely wealthy and some even respectable, like **Henry Morgan** (1635–88), whose buccaneer career was crowned by a knighthood and the governorship of the island of Jamaica.

Port Royal's glory days ended 7 June 1692, however, when it was struck by a severe earthquake, followed by tidal waves which inundated most of the city.

▲ *Above: Sugar cultivation and slavery went hand in hand for centuries.*

Sugar and Slaves

By the 18th century, Europeans had recognised that the wealth of the Caribbean was not in gold but in **sugar**, which could be grown in huge quantities on the uncultivated soil of Jamaica and which commanded high prices in Europe, where there was an insatiable market. By the time of the British settlement, the Arawaks had already been almost annihilated. Attempts to work the cane-fields using indentured European labourers and Irish, Scottish and English **prisoners** of various civil wars and rebellions proved impracticable, as most quickly fell victim to disease. The solution was to import huge numbers of **slaves** from **West Africa**, ushering in one of the most shameful eras of oppression in history.

Sugar boomed, and Jamaica became one of the richest farming colonies. But the cost of human life for this new wealth was immense. During the 18th century more than 600,000 slaves were brought to Jamaica. One in five died during the Atlantic crossing, and Africans fell

SLAVERY

The British started growing sugar in **Barbados**, but the conquest of Jamaica opened up a new frontier of unimaginable wealth. By the 1740s there were almost 500 sugar plantations on the island and Jamaica was the world's biggest sugar producer.

victim to local diseases as easily as Europeans. For every child born in slavery, six slaves died. Not surprisingly, slaves frequently sought to escape the brutal life on the plantations and succeeded in reaching freedom in the jungle fortresses of Maroon territory. Punishments for disobedience or attempted escape were unimaginably vicious, and execution by torture was routine. But life as a slave was so grim that even the most savage penalties failed to prevent repeated rebellions.

The fiercely independent Maroons remained a thorn in the side of the British. As early as 1690, they joined forces with rebel slaves in an island-wide rising that became known as the **First Maroon War**. The rebellion started among the slaves of the Clarendon area, most of whom were **Coromantee** from what is now Ghana. With the help of his brothers, **Accompong** and **Johnny**, and other Maroon chiefs such as **Cuffee** and **Quao**, the charismatic leader **Cudjoe** led a resistance for almost half a century. Eventually, the British brought in Indian trackers from the Mosquito Coast of Central America. One by one the Maroon villages were discovered and homes and fields burnt. On 31 March 1739, Cudjoe signed a treaty of friendship which set aside 1500 acres of land for the Maroons, and confirmed Cudjoe and his brothers as their rulers under the British crown, but bound them to return escaped slaves and to support the British against slave rebellions.

There were, however, subsequent slave rebellions. In 1760, a Coromantee leader named **Tacky** led hundreds of slaves in a revolt which proved hard to quell – even with the help of the Maroons – and there were many smaller risings. In 1795 there was a second war with the Maroons, sparked by the flogging of two Maroons for stealing a pig. The war lasted for six months until the governor, the Earl of Balcarres, brought in a contingent of killer dogs and their handlers from Cuba. Defeated, 600 Maroons were deported to Nova Scotia and, although those who remained were treated fairly leniently, Maroon power was finally broken.

MARCUS MOSIAH GARVEY

Marcus Mosiah Garvey (1887–1940) founded his **Universal Negro Improvement Association** to give the descendants of African slaves a new pride in their African roots, calling for Africans in the Caribbean and the Americas, and in the European colonies in Africa, to unite and rely on each other, not on whites. Urging African-Americans to go back to Africa to try to build a new world there, Garvey tried to set up his own ocean liner company, the **Black Star Line**, but his search for investors led to his imprisonment for mail fraud – almost certainly unjustly. He died in exile in London, but is buried in Jamaica, where he is a national hero.

▼ *Below: A statue at St Ann's Bay of black leader Marcus Garvey.*

SLAVERY

Growing, harvesting and processing sugar cane is still brutally hard work, and in the 18th and 19th centuries, before mechanisation, was even harder – so hard, in fact, that no volunteer labour could be found. Sugar in industrial quantities could not be profitably produced with free labour. The plantations give the lie to the proverb that 'hard work never killed anybody' – it killed hundreds of thousands of slaves.

In the end, the abolition of slavery was largely driven by economics and politics. Demand for sugar was down, the price had dropped, and the plantation lobby's political influence was in eclipse. Freedom for a slave, however, rarely meant freedom from want. For many, life after emancipation remained just as hard.

Abolition

The beginning of the end of the dark era of slavery came in 1807, when Britain not only abolished British trade in slaves from Africa but set out to end the trade entirely. But the strength of the sugar lobby in Parliament and the conviction that the sugar plantations could be worked only by slave labour helped slavery survive in Jamaica until 1834.

The demise of slavery was hastened by the massive slave revolt of December 1831. Led by a Baptist minister named **Sam 'Daddy' Sharpe**, some 20,000 slaves rose in the Montego Bay area. They were persuaded to surrender peacefully when the British governor prematurely announced that slavery had been abolished by Parliament, but Sharpe and more than 1000 of his followers were nevertheless executed. Public opinion in Britain, which by then was strongly against slavery, was outraged and in 1834 slavery was finally abolished by Act of Parliament.

After Slavery

In some ways, life was even harder for black Jamaicans after abolition. Plantation owners no longer had the power to flog and torture at will, but all political and economic power remained in the hands of a tiny white ruling class. Though free, former slaves had to find shelter and sustenance for themselves, and there were few jobs outside the plantations, where many former slaves found themselves working for tiny wages under conditions not much better than those experienced during the days of slavery. Poverty was widespread and was made harsher by the American Civil War, when the southern states – which supplied much of Jamaica's food – were blockaded by the US Navy.

▼ *Below: Sam Sharpe leads 20,000 slaves in the rebellion of 1831.*

In October 1865, hunger and social injustice prompted the **Morant Bay Rebellion** by black Jamaicans demanding fairer treatment. The uprising was crushed with the usual savagery: some 430 rebels were hanged, hundreds more were flogged, and the leaders, **George William Gordon** and **Paul Bogle**, executed for treason. Both are today national heroes.

▲ *Above: A mural in Morant Bay depicts the brutal ending of the 1865 uprising.*

However, the Morant Bay Rebellion had one positive result, persuading the white planters who ran the ruling Assembly to accept a slightly more enlightened Crown Colony government. Through the later 1800s, British governors reformed Jamaica's political and judicial systems, created a modern police force on British lines, and introduced minimum standards of health, education and welfare. Sugar was no longer all-important, and banana growing – which began in the late 19th century – quickly became a major part of the economy. Nevertheless, from the point of view of most Jamaicans, the colony remained a place of great economic, political and racial inequality.

The world depression of the 1930s brought even greater hardship and triggered island-wide riots. From this period of dissatisfaction emerged Jamaica's first home-grown political and workers' movements. **Alexander Bustamante's Industrial Trade Union** later spawned the centre-right **Jamaica Labour Party** (JLP). On the political left, **Norman Manley** founded the socialist **People's National Party** (PNP), which came to be allied to the **Jamaica Trades Union Congress** and the **National Workers' Union**. From the early '40s these rival movements were in the vanguard of the broad campaign for better pay and conditions, wider political rights for Jamaicans, and eventual full independence. In 1944 voting rights were given to all adults.

GEORGE GORDON

George William Gordon (1810–165), son of a white farmer, was the first black Jamaican to be elected to Jamaica's colonial legislature. A lay preacher, he campaigned for the hundreds of thousands of Jamaicans left to fend for themselves after the end of the plantation system. He was caught up in the **Morant Bay Rebellion** of 1865, and executed as one of its leaders. Gordon appears to have been innocent, and his execution a convenient way of ridding the white ruling class of a thorn in its flesh. Today, like other historic resistance leaders including the Maroon chiefs **Nanny** and **Cudjoe**, **Paul Bogle** and **Sam Sharpe**, he is a national hero.

▲ *Above: Montego Bay's airport is named after former leader Donald Sangster.*

Constitutional Change

Changes to the constitution in the 1950s culminated in internal self-government by an elected Jamaican cabinet in 1959, and in full independence on 6 August 1962. Jamaica's first free elections catapulted Alexander Bustamante and the JLP to power.

Firmly aligned with the capitalist world and committed to close ties with Britain and the Commonwealth, the JLP remained in power under Bustamante until 1967, and then for a further five years under his successors, **Donald Sangster** and **Hugh Shearer**. Eventually, the electorate decided it was time for a change. A rising population, ramshackle economy, poor infrastructure, urban and rural poverty, and high unemployment contributed to a landslide victory for the left-wing PNP in 1972. Led by **Michael Manley**, charismatic firebrand son of the PNP's founder, Jamaica moved closer to the non-aligned Third World, outlining ambitious plans for social reform. Sadly for Jamaica, the PNP achieved few of its aims despite almost a decade in power. Terrified by Manley's leftist rhetoric, foreign investors took their capital elsewhere, as did many better-off Jamaicans. The economy went into a nose-dive, foreign exchange reserves collapsed, and shortages of everyday goods became common. The US government, angry with the PNP's flirtation with socialist Cuba, painted Manley as a second Fidel Castro, and many on the left of Jamaican politics still see the hidden hand of destabilisation experts of the US Central Intelligence Agency behind the economic and political catastrophes of the 1970s.

The Modern Era

Politically motivated violence declined after the JLP, led by Edward Seaga, won the 1979 election. Despite a decade in power, Seaga's free-market capitalism did

CRIME AND PUNISHMENT

Jamaica's murder rate more than doubled between 1998 and 2008, with 1600 slayings in 2008. Jamaica's police commissioner vowed to reduce the number of killings by 5 per cent in 2009, by setting up task forces to take gang leaders and 'shottas' (gunmen) off the streets. In 2004, Jamaica's highest court ruled that the mandatory death sentence for murder was unconstitutional. However, in December 2008 both houses of the Jamaican Parliament voted to bring back hanging. Opponents argue that there is no evidence that the death penalty acts as a deterrent, and that Jamaica's crime problem can only be tackled by better policing. In March 2008, the human rights group Jamaicans For Justice claimed 20 per cent of killings were 'extra-judicial executions' by police officers.

nothing to resolve Jamaica's problems and the PNP returned to power in 1989. Michael Manley retired from politics in 1993, and was succeeded by PJ Patterson, who in turn stepped down as PNP leader and PM in 2006 and was succeeded by Portia Simpson-Miller, Jamaica's first woman premier. Fifteen years of PNP rule ended in 2007, when Bruce Golding led the JLP to a narrow victory, winning a six-seat majority with just over 50 per cent of the vote – only 2940 votes more than the PNP. Several independent candidates and smaller parties – including the National Democratic Movement, the United People Party, the Republican Party and the Imperial Ethiopian World Federation Incorporation Party, the Jamaica Alliance Movement and the Jerusalem Bread Foundation – also contested the election, without winning any seats. Elections are next due by October 2012.

GOVERNMENT AND ECONOMY

Jamaica is a member of the Commonwealth, with its own constitution and political institutions. A two-chamber **Parliament** consists of an elected **House of Representatives** and a **Senate** whose members are jointly appointed by the prime minister and the leader of the opposition. Elections are held every five years, but Queen Elizabeth II remains ceremonial head of state, represented by a governor-general who is traditionally a distinguished Jamaican appointed by the prime minister. At local govern-ment level, Jamaica is divided into three counties (Cornwall, Middlesex and Surrey) and these, in turn, are divided into a total of 14 **parishes** – all with distinctly English names – which are administered by elected councils. Jamaica is a

TOURISM

Tourism came to Jamaica in the early 1900s when **Captain Lorenzo Dow Baker** realised he could bring visitors from chilly North America to **Port Antonio** in his fleet of banana boats. World War II put Europe off limits to wealthy Americans, making Jamaica even more popular. After the war, tourism flourished, but took a dip with the political violence of the 70s. Recovery began as cheaper flights brought new waves of visitors from Europe. All-inclusive resorts, conceived in the 80s, have since boomed, offering security and value for money – but mostly cocooning their guests from the real Jamaica.

▼ Below: A cruise ship lies off Ocho Rios, a hub of tourism in Jamaica.

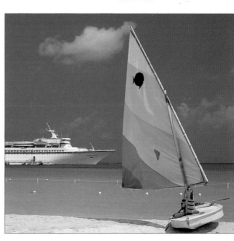

strongly partisan country, and political grumbling is part of the Jamaican way of life, with supporters of each side frequently and vocally accusing rival politicos of corruption, fraud, cynicism and incompetence.

Economic Development

Jamaica has suffered continuing economic decline since 2008, and its economy faces problems including a major trade deficit (driven by the cost of importing fuel, foodstuffs and manufactured products), high inflation, and large public debt. The cost of servicing bailouts for the financial sector in the late 1990s accounts for almost half of government spending and hampers government investment in public services and infrastructure. Unemployment is around 10%. Underemployment is also an issue. Around 15% of Jamaicans are reckoned to live below the poverty line. In 2008 Jamaica signed an Economic Partnership Agreement with the EU, but Europe's own economic problems mean this has so far failed to usher in a new era of prosperity.

Industry and Agriculture

Tourism is the country's biggest foreign currency earner and one of its major employers, with an annual turnover of close to US$ 900 million. Many Jamaicans are ambivalent about the holiday industry. Although they recognise that it brings much-needed cash and jobs, they object to being treated as a nation of waiters, bar staff and taxi drivers. Second to tourism is **bauxite mining**, with bauxite ore bringing in around 40 per cent of export earnings.

▶ *Opposite: Though illegal, marijuana plantations are not an unusual sight.*
▼ *Below: Prospect Plantation – The Great House.*

Sugar cane is the most important crop and the country's biggest employer, but **bananas**, **cocoa** and **coffee** are also rather important revenue earners. **Wages** for this kind of work are low, and many people earn as little as US$20 per week. Imported and manufactured goods are expensive, even by British or US standards. Jamaica must import all its **fuel** and, as the Jamaican dollar declines steadily against the US dollar, this only adds to the country's economic problems.

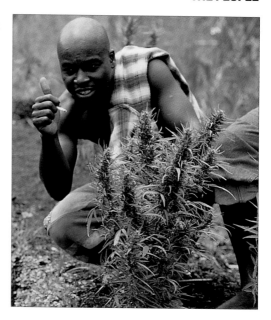

Since the early 1980s, Jamaican authorities have tacitly – and sometimes openly – admitted that the illegal trade in **ganja** (marijuana) has become an important part of the economy. In Jamaica's steamy tropical climate, ganja grows profusely even on poor soil which will support no other cash crops. Some sources have estimated that the ganja business is worth as much as US$1 billion a year, outstripping all legitimate sectors of the economy. Arguably, legalisation could bring the country's economic woes to an end overnight, but the predictably violent reaction from the US precludes any such move.

THE PEOPLE

One in three of Jamaica's 2.8 million people lives in Kingston, with around 300,000 scattered around the island's other main towns and villages. Around 95 per cent of Jamaicans are black descendants of **African** slaves, although skin tones range from very dark to very light, and there are small **Indian**, **Lebanese** and **Chinese** minorities. Since the tourist-deterring troubles of the

COFFEE

Jamaica produces the world's finest – and most expensive coffee. On the slopes of the **Blue Mountains**, some 4000 farms produce up to 15,000 bushels of Blue Mountain beans a year. The arabica coffee grown here originated in **Ethiopia** and was brought over via **Martinique** in 1728. Today, the right to use the Blue Mountain name is strictly controlled, with the best of the crop grown above the 2000ft (6560m) mark. But you'll be lucky to be served Blue Mountain coffee in Jamaica – almost all is exported to Japan, where it fetches incredibly high prices.

INTRODUCING JAMAICA

JAMAICANS OVERSEAS

A combination of poverty, energy and high aspirations has driven many Jamaicans overseas in search of better jobs and living conditions than they find at home. There are large communities of first-, second- and third-generation Jamaicans in the UK, the USA and Canada, and nearer to home several thousand Jamaicans work in the Cayman Islands. Many are high achievers in their adopted homes, not only as musicians and athletes – traditional routes out of the ghetto – but as professionals, statesmen and even military supremos such as **General Colin Powell**, former head of the US Chiefs of Staff.

late 1970s, the Jamaican Tourist Board has spent millions stressing the warmth and friendliness of the Jamaican people. On first acquaintance, though, most visitors find Jamaicans rather more reserved than initially imagined. Eliciting a smile from a Jamaican barman, bank teller or shop assistant is an achievement. Sometimes, it can be as difficult to attract the attention of a waiter as to avoid the attentions of beach hustlers, black-market money changers and small-time drug dealers, all of whom may become abusive if you politely refuse their offers.

The huge gap between your disposable income and that of the Jamaicans who serve you accounts, for a large part, for this behaviour. That said, many visitors perceive Jamaicans as aggressive simply because of the direct way they express themselves. A souvenir pedlar is more likely to seek your attention with 'You! Come 'ere!' than with a polite 'Excuse me'.

Language

Although Jamaica's language is officially **English**, it takes no more than a few sentences for the visitor to realise that Jamaican **patois** is quite different from any other Anglo-Saxon dialect. Jamaicans are comfortable in both 'standard' English – flavoured with American and British influences – and their own spicy, incomprehensible dialect. The richly creative Jamaican patois is still evolving, with its own distinct grammar and syntax, and its vocabulary features numerous loanwords from West African languages and other sources as disparate as Gaelic, Spanish and 17th-century English. Patois is clearly on its way to

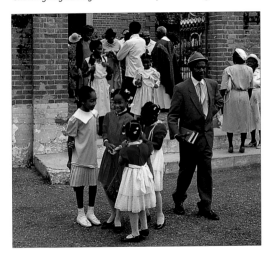

▼ *Below: Sunday worship is a regular occasion in this church-going society.*

becoming an authentic language in its own right, and there are serious proposals that the Jamaican government should recognise the language as a second national language.

Religion

Jamaican life juxtaposes a bawdy tolerance with a dignified conservatism. On the one hand, it is common for both men and women to have children by several partners; there are more ganja smokers than abstainers; and the 'slack' verses of today's reggae and dub musicians revel in explicit sexual detail. On the other hand, every settlement – no matter how tiny – has at least one church, and Sunday worship is an occasion for formal wear and staid behaviour – no matter how raucous the preceding Saturday night. The **Anglican Church of Jamaica** is the most widespread denomination, with substantial numbers of **Roman Catholic** worshippers and a myriad of smaller **Protestant** churches.

Jamaica's unique home-grown religion, **Rasta-farianism**, is a rather complicated brew of Old Testament Christianity, ganja-fuelled mysticism, revealed truth and back-to-Africa fundamentalism. 'Rastas' wear their hair in long, matted dreadlocks, venerate the former Emperor of Ethiopia, **Haile Selassie**, and aim to live a contemplative life away from the temptations and tribulations of the modern, urban 'Babylon'. It is a major religion in Jamaica and includes various sects. Some followers have even emigrated to Ethiopia, regarded as the source of their religion. But, at times, true Rastafarians may seem to be outnumbered by those for whom the lion-like mane is a style statement rather than the expression of a deeply held belief.

▲ *Above: A Kingstonian takes time out to enjoy a cool beer.*

OBEAH

In Haiti it's called **voodoo**, in the Dominican Republic **santeria**, and in Jamaica it is known as **obeah**. Under any name, it is a surviving, much-altered relic of the original animist religions of West Africa, with its practitioners appealing to a host of deities to intercede on their behalf. Brought over and covertly maintained by African slaves and their descendants well into the mid-19th century, obeah is said to be used clandestinely to this day, to bring both good and bad luck.

Art and Culture

Like many fledgling nations, Jamaica took time to find its artistic feet. Until well into the 20th century, the cultural roots of the majority of its people were ignored, suppressed, or regarded as second-rate, and the imported European traditions of the white plantocracy prevailed. From the 1920s onwards, though, a truly Jamaican artistic movement was born. The works of many of its founders can be seen today in the National Gallery of Jamaica in Kingston, perhaps the finest art collection in the Caribbean region, and paintings and carvings by their successors can be bought at excellent private galleries in Kingston and all over the island. Look out for works by the late **Edna Manley** (wife of PNP founder Norman Manley and mother of the former prime minister Michael Manley), whose powerful carvings – many of them with strong political and social messages – put her at the forefront of this Jamaican cultural revolution. One of her last works, *The Voice*, is a tribute to the late Bob Marley, the man who brought Jamaica's own music to the world stage.

Truly original artists from this first new wave of Jamaican creativity include **Shepherd Kapo**, whose powerful, quasi-religious paintings of visions and illusionary landscapes as well as his remarkable carvings adorn their own section of the National Gallery; the naturalistic painter **Albert Huie**; and the sculptor **Alvin Marriott**. In 1950, the **Jamaica School of Art** was set up to become the nexus for development of a Jamaican artistic tradition, and in 1976 it became part of the newly created **Kingston Cultural Training Centre**, which comprises schools of art, music, dance and drama.

As well as the work of its mainstream artists, Jamaica abounds in talented, self-taught artists whose carvings and colourful paintings can be bought at very affordable prices in galleries and craft markets around the island's main resorts. Naive and imitative though these works often are, the best of them radiate a brilliance of colour and a raw, youthful energy that is truly Jamaican, and make excellent souvenirs of your Jamaican holiday.

A gleaming new arts venue, the **Simon Bolivar Cultural Centre**, is due to open in 2011 in Kingston, built with a US$294 million investment from the Venezuelan Economic and Social Development Bank (BANDES).

Music

Music is probably Jamaica's best-known export. Since stars like **Jimmy Cliff**, **Toots and The Maytals** and, above all, **Bob Marley and The Wailers**, took **reggae** out of the ghetto and into the world album charts more than 20 years ago, the distinctive, rather slow-moving beat and throbbing bass of Jamaican music have travelled the world.

Reggae emerged in the early 1970s (**Frederick Hibbert** of Toots and The Maytals is credited with inventing the name), the latest mutation in a long line of descent from traditional melodies and rhythms brought to Jamaica by enslaved Africans. Deprived of material possessions and robbed of their native languages and traditions – and even of their names – music was the only memory of Africa the slaves could keep, and must have been especially precious.

African rhythms contributed to the invention of the slow and sensual musical style called

◄ *Opposite: Colourful designs like this batik hoopoe bird are common.*
▼ *Below: Dreadlocks and reggae are both distinctive Jamaican exports.*

▲ Above: Slick entertainment at the Grand Lido resort near Negril.

mento which reigned supreme until the 1950s, when the sound of the USA started to dominate Jamaican airwaves. Influenced by jazz, rhythm and blues drifting over the Caribbean from New Orleans and points north, Jamaican musicians invented their own variation on the theme. This they called ska, a rather fast-moving, mostly instrumental dance rhythm which was subsequently carried to Britain by migrant Jamaicans. But it was reggae, evolving out of ska by way of a slower sound called 'rock steady', that really caught the world's imagination.

Reggae's first exponents included established musicians such as Frederick 'Toots' Hibbert, Jimmy Cliff and **Desmond Decker**. However, it took four boys from the streets of Kingston's Trench Town ghetto to take reggae worldwide.

As the Wailing Rude Boys – and later The Wailers – **Bob Marley**, **Bunny 'Wailer' Livingstone**, **Peter 'Tosh' MacIntosh** and **Junior Braithwaite** wrote and performed their own songs, many of them expressing discontent and protest, that struck a chord not only in Jamaica but worldwide. And you could dance to them. In the mid-1970s reggae exploded onto the international music scene and began to influence established jazz and rock musicians all over the world. Since then it has never gone away.

Reggae's current exponents keep the flame alight, while Jamaican music continued its evolution into forms like **dancehall,** with its 'chattering' DJs interacting with their audiences, and **ragga** (ragamuffin), both of which owe an enormous debt to reggae.

PATOIS

To the untrained ear, Jamaican patois does not sound even faintly like English. Most Jamaicans, whether fishermen, farmers or Harvard-trained businessmen, switch fluently from Caribbean-accented standard English when talking to foreigners into their own impenetrable dialect when talking to each other, and for many younger middle-class Jamaicans fluency in the patois is essential to their street credibility. Long neglected and even looked down upon, patois is beginning to receive recognition as both a language in its own right and central to the nation's culture, with many Jamaican **poets** and **authors** following in the footsteps of **reggae** musicians to use it in their own work.

Film

Fabulous landscapes, perfect weather, close proximity to the USA and a long tradition of tax breaks for foreign film production companies have made Jamaica a favourite location for many well-loved movies, from the golden years of Hollywood (when, led by Errol Flynn, many stars sojourned on the island) to the heyday of the James Bond films (Bond's creator, Ian Fleming, had a home near Ocho Rios). Home-made films starring Jamaican artists are fewer, but one in particular deserves mention because it played a big part in launching reggae onto the world stage. *The Harder They Come*, starring musician Jimmy Cliff as a fiercely ambitious ghetto kid bent on fame, and with an exhaustive soundtrack featuring tracks by Cliff, The Maytals, and Desmond Decker, remains a cult classic.

Sport and Recreation

Jamaicans – and its men especially – take an enthusiastic interest in sport. **Cricket** is a runaway favourite, and Jamaicans follow the fortunes of national players and the West Indies team with near-religious fervour. Jamaica's world-class athletics stars include Usain 'Lightning' Bolt, who won three gold medals at the 2008 Olympic Games in Beijing and set new world records for the 100 metres, 200 metres and 100 metres relay, and Shelly-Ann Fraser – nicknamed the 'Pocket Rocket' for her diminutive size – who struck gold in the women's 100 metres. Veronica Campbell-Brown won another gold for Jamaica in the women's 200 metres and Melanie Walker took yet another in the women's 400-metre hurdles.

Soccer is an even more popular everyday pastime, though it does not feature high on Jamaica's sporting calendar as an organised sport and Jamaica has only just begun to make its mark internationally.

Robert Nesta Marley (1940–81) took Jamaican **reggae** music to a world audience. Born at **Nine Mile**, near Runaway Bay, he moved with his family to the **Trench Town** ghetto area of Kingston at 13. By his late teens he was already making music, with a band called **The Wailers**. Though his fellow-Wailers were fine musicians, Marley's songwriting flair and soaring voice lifted the band above the run-of-the-mill competition. In 1978, Marley was shot by four gunmen at his Kingston home, but survived to host a concert which brought prime minister Michael Manley and opposition leader Eddie Seaga together to urge – unsuccessfully – an end to the current violence. His death from brain cancer was tragically early.

◄ Left: Most famous of all Jamaica's musicians, Bob Marley lives on in memory.

CRICKET

Cricket is more than a national pastime in Jamaica; it's a national obsession. Thousands pack Kingston's **Sabina Park** when Jamaica plays other Caribbean nations, or when the **West Indies** meets England, Australia, New Zealand or South Africa. Jamaican boys have bat and ball in hand as soon as they can walk, and any piece of flat ground in town or village is used as a makeshift pitch as soon as school or church is out. In a nation which lives in the shadow of the USA and which is still inventing its own identity, cricket is the most visible and longest lasting of Jamaica's links with the UK, and even the flood of US sports such as baseball, basketball and gridiron football on satellite television show little sign of dimming Jamaica's passionate love affair with cricket.

For the visitor, Jamaica is a holiday destination rich in sporting activities, ranging from **golf** on some of the world's top courses – such as Tryall, home of golf's biggest prize event, the World Championship – to **tennis**, **riding**, **deep-sea fishing** for marlin, wahoo and tuna, and a wide range of **water sports**.

Food and Drink

Jamaica's culinary tradition is heavy on calories and even heavier on spicy flavourings. But be sure to sample **jerk** chicken, beef, pork or fish – marinated in a piquant mix of hot peppers, pimento, spices, thyme,

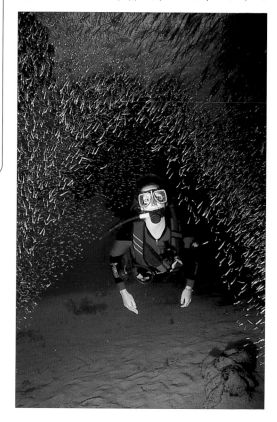

▶ Right: Immensely popular with divers from all around the world, the Caribbean's waters are warm and teem with marine life such as silversides; top of the list of places to dive is almost certainly the Cayman Islands, but Jamaica's coastline also includes several stretches of healthy coral reef.

and onions, and grilled over fragrant barbecue coals of allspice wood. Equally spicy is **curry goat**, eaten with rice on special occasions, or meat-filled **Jamaica patties** stuffed with flavoured chicken or beef mince. Kidney beans (known as 'red peas') appear in **red pea soup**, a blend of beef, beans, and onions flavoured with

▲ Above: Jamaican ackee and saltfish.

peppers, thyme and garlic, and in **red peas and rice**, the Jamaican chef's favourite filler. **Ackee**, a red, pod-like fruit which when cooked is almost indistinguishable from perfectly scrambled egg, is usually flavoured with salt cod, another Jamaican favourite, or bacon. Other vegetables include **calalloo**, a spinach-like leaf served as a side dish or in **pepperpot soup**, which also features yam, peppers, coconut milk, and beef. Delicious fruit includes **pineapple**, star apple **sweetsop** and, of course, **coconut**, the milk of which is an essential ingredient in dozens of delicious cocktails.

Jamaican rum, distilled from sugar cane by makers including the Appleton and Wray & Nephew distilleries, is renowned for its subtle potency. Gold rum, aged in oak barrels, can be mellow enough to sip after dinner, while white rum is more suitable with mixers or as a base for cocktails. Jamaican overproof rum, with a proof rating of up to 140 degrees, is arguably more suitable for use as rocket fuel than as a drink. Coffee-flavoured **Tia Maria** liqueur, another Jamaican original, is a delicious after-dinner drink, while on a hot afternoon on the beach an ice cold **Red Stripe** lager, brewed by Desnoes and Geddes, is guaranteed to hit the spot.

JAMAICAN DISHES

Everybody has to try **jerk**, but there are lots of other Jamaican dishes on the menu. Try **festival**, a fried cornmeal dumpling, or **breadfruit** – boiled or roasted – to go with your jerk meat. **Bammy**, a round flat bread made from grated cassava (a yam-like root from South America) goes well with fish. **Johnny cakes** are fried dumplings, **callaloo** is a spinach-like vegetable, and **patties** – pitta-like meat pies stuffed with spicy beef, chicken or fish – are a meal in themselves. If you are wondering what gives Jamaican jerk seasoning its legendary bite, the culprit is 'scotch bonnet' – one of the most formidable chilli peppers to be found.

2
Kingston and St Andrew

Jamaica's capital lies on the south coast and boasts one of the most striking locations of any city in the world. Kingston stretches inland from the **Caribbean** towards the spectacular inland scenery of the **Blue Mountains**, which dominate the capital's northern skyline. A sprawling urban centre of more than 800,000 people – almost one-third of Jamaica's total population – Kingston seems to have little in common with the laid-back resorts on the island's best beaches, or with the small fishing villages of Jamaica's coasts and mountains.

Kingston is Jamaica's second capital. The first, **Spanish Town** – centre of the first Spanish settlement – lies some 10 miles (16km) west of Kingston, and is likely to be eventually absorbed by Kingston's urban sprawl. **Port Royal**, the infamous buccaneer's lair which was demolished by a giant earthquake in 1692, lies just across Kingston Harbour and can be seen from the Kingston waterfront.

As your plane makes its approach into **Norman Manley International Airport** it is easy to see why Spaniards, pirates and British governors favoured this part of the island. The airport is located on a long spur of land which stretches from the mainland, with Port Royal at its western tip. **Kingston Harbour**, sheltered by this narrow peninsula, is the finest anchorage in the Caribbean, and one of the largest natural harbours in the world – which is precisely why successive occupiers made this area their Caribbean headquarters, and why rival powers such as France so keenly sought to evict the British from Jamaica.

CARIBBEAN SEA

◄ *Opposite: Devon House is one of Jamaica's finest buildings.*

CLIMATE

Kingston can get very **hot**. Coastal temperatures tend to average 28°C (82°F), with a maximum of 32°C (90°F) and a minimum of 27°C (49°F). Although the south coast receives less rain than the north, there is always the possibility of tropical storms and downpours during Jul–Oct.

Kingston was founded in the early 1690s, following the destruction of Port Royal, but became the capital only in 1872, when the seat of government was relocated from Spanish Town. Successive fires, and another earthquake in 1907, have left relatively few older buildings standing amid more recent residential and commercial building, most of it constructed from the 1950s and 60s onward.

Kingston has a throbbing street life, with busy markets (almost every downtown street has 'higglers' or street vendors) and an even hotter nightlife. Cultural venues include the 1000-seat **Ward Theatre** and also the 600-seat **Little Theatre**, which host performances by the **National Dance Theatre Company**, the **National Chorale** and the **Jamaica Philharmonic Symphony Orchestra** as well as reggae which may be heard in dozens of the city's night-spots.

North of the city, where the foothills of the Blue Mountains offer cooling breezes, plush residential suburbs house some of Kingston's wealthier residents. Straddling St Andrew, Portland and St Thomas parishes, the **Blue Mountains** rise to a height of 7402ft (2256m). The marvellous Blue Mountains–John Crow Mountains national parks offer a growing network of hiking trails.

DOWNTOWN KINGSTON

Many of Kingston's oldest colonial buildings and land-marks, as well as a string of modern banks, corporate headquarters and several of the city's main tourist attractions, are close to the harbour waterfront. There also two museums of note.

National Gallery ★★★

Situated in the Roy West Building at Kingston Mall (12 Ocean Boulevard, Kingston), the National Gallery's collection includes pieces by artists such as **Joseph Kidd** and **George Robertson**, whose work comprises portraits of governors, generals and wealthy planters of the colonial era as well as island landscapes. These, however, are outshone by the much more vital and exciting works of 20th-century Jamaican artists, notably the outstanding sculptures of **Edna Manley**. A common theme in Manley's work is the need for Jamaicans to feel dignity and pride in themselves, from works like *The Diggers*, dating from the 1930s, to the powerful depiction of Bob Marley, *The Voice*, which has pride of place, guitar in one hand and finger pointed heavenward. The gallery also has a fine collection of the work of the revivalist painter and woodcarver **Shepherd Kapo**. Also worth looking out for are the works of artists such as **Leonard Daley**, **Albert Artwell**, and **Everald Brown** who have taken much of their inspiration from Rastafarianism. Open Tue–Thu 10:00–16:30, Fri 10:00–16:00, Sat 10:00–15:00.

Institute of Jamaica (and African Caribbean Institute) ★

At 10–16 East Street is this collection of tools, utensils, musical instruments and other artefacts which cast an interesting sidelight on Jamaican history from the

▼ *Below: Ocean Boulevard contains a string of corporate headquarters, and the National Gallery.*

HIGGLERS AND HUSTLERS

For many, if not most Jamaicans, life is a matter of making it as best you can, and the crowds of **hustlers** who greet you as soon as you step into the airport arrivals hall are prime examples of the Jamaican hustler, who you'll meet at every turn offering a range of goods and services from straw hats and parasail rides to transportation and illicit substances. They can persist, but a firm but polite refusal will eventually deter them. **Higglers** – the stalwart ladies who dominate most Jamaican marketplaces – are worthy adversaries for even the most skilled negotiator, and you'll be lucky to get the better of the amiable bargaining involved in buying anything from them.

point of view of its African Caribbean people. Founded in 1879, the Institute also houses Jamaica's national **archives**, with the largest **reference library** documenting the history of the Caribbean anywhere in the world. The Institute is at the very heart of Jamaica's cultural scene, housing the **Cultural Training Centre**, which includes the national schools of art, dance and drama, and the **African Caribbean Institute**, a centre for research into cultural and traditional links between Africa and Jamaica and other Caribbean nations. Open Monday–Friday 09:00–16:30 (www.instituteofjamaica.org.jm).

Crafts Market ★★

On the waterfront at Port Royal Street, the crafts market offers typical Jamaican souvenir shopping – linens, silk and cotton batik **textiles**, **wood carvings**, colourful woven **baskets** and vibrant naive **paintings** of rural and urban life. That said, the Kingston market is far from unique. There are similar crafts markets at other resort centres, including Negril, Montego Bay and Ocho Rios, so if you are staying elsewhere on the island and your time in Kingston is limited, you may want to give this market a fairly low priority. Open 07:00–18:00 Monday–Saturday. (When this edition was updated in 2011, the Crafts Market faced closure due to health risks associated with its elderly and crumbling asbestos roof.)

Kingston Parish Church ★★

The original Kingston Parish Church on the corner of King Street and South Parade was built in the late 17th century, as indicated by a tombstone in its churchyard dated 1699. Destroyed in the 1907 earthquake, the 1911 building which now stands in its place is a copy of the original building. Just like London's Cockneys, city-dwellers claim that the only true Kingstonians – a breed now heavily outnumbered by migrants from the countryside – are people born 'under the clock', or within earshot of the Parish Church bell. The bell is housed in a square clocktower, and was cast for the first Parish Church in 1715, surprisingly surviving the earthquake. Open daily.

◀ *Left: The Hilton Kingston Hotel is located in the heart of the city.*

Ward Theatre ★★

On the Parade on the north side of the pleasant William Grant Park stands the impressive Ward Theatre. Its pale blue-and-white colonial baroque frontage makes this one of Kingston's most attractive older buildings. Given to the city by **Colonel Charles Ward**, it opened in 1911 and, after closing for renovation in 2007, is scheduled to reopen in 2012 after a US$6.2 million refurbishment.

Gordon House ★

Built in 1960, Gordon House is named after **George William Gordon**, who was executed after the Morant Bay rebellion of 1865 and is now remembered as one of Jamaica's most prominent national heroes. It is the seat of Jamaica's **House of Representatives**, and British visitors in particular will notice a close resemblance to the interior design and protocol of Westminster Palace's House of Commons – though the resemblance does not extend to the building's exterior. Visits are by appointment only.

NEW KINGSTON AND OLD HOPE ROAD

Between Hope Road and Old Hope Road lies New Kingston, home to most of the city's international hotels. The area also contains a fair number of embassies, government buildings and offices. To the east along the Old Hope Road are the historic Hope Botanical Gardens.

BRITISH RELICS

Jamaica is completely independent of the UK, but relics of British rule abound, from elderly British-made **Morris** and **Oxford** cars still clanking around the streets of Kingston (and driving on the left) to the grand ceremonial which surrounds the office of **Governor General** or the British military-style dress uniforms worn by **Jamaican policemen**, complete with broad red stripe down the side of the trousers. The portrait of **Queen Elizabeth II** on every Jamaican dollar and cent is another reminder of links with the colonial power.

▲ *Above: Built for Jamaica's earliest black millionaire, Devon House has an interesting history.*

HALF WAY TREE

All over Jamaica you will see the towering **kapok** tree, easily identified by the fluffy white fibres (used for stuffing cushions and soft furnishings) which explode from its seed pods. In central Kingston, **Half Way Tree** marks the spot where one mighty specimen became a landmark for early settlers. Once midway between Kingston and the market gardens of the nearby hills, it is now in the very heart of the urban sprawl.

Devon House ★★★

This immaculately restored mansion at 26 Hope Road dates from 1881, when it was built for Jamaica's first black millionaire, shipwright **George Stiebel**. Stiebel's fortune was made not in Jamaica, where people of African descent were still at a great disadvantage during the 19th century, but in South America, and the elegant home he commissioned on his return was clearly designed to show off his hard-earned wealth. Furnished with 19th-century antiques, the house, with its arcade of white pillars supporting a pretty first-floor balcony, is one of Jamaica's most handsome buildings. Its outbuildings now house some attractive arts, crafts and antique shops as well as two pleasant restaurants. Open 09:30–17:00 Tuesday–Saturday (www.devonhousejamaica.com).

King's House and Jamaica House ★★

Massive wrought-iron gates just off Hope Road mark the entrance to the vast landscaped grounds which enclose **King's House**, residence of the Governor General, and Jamaica House, the executive office of the prime minister. The Governor General of Jamaica is the Queen's official representative on the island and is chosen by appointment from among the ranks of the island's dignitaries. King's House stands on the site of the Bishop's Lodge, the residence of the Bishop of Jamaica, which was destroyed in 1907 by an earthquake. Rebuilt to a design by the English architect Sir Charles Nicholson, it now has a grace and dignity which befit its role and is enhanced by the 200 acres of beautiful surrounding tropical gardens. King's House was refurbished from top to bottom in 1995–96 and is now a marvellous setting for its collections of antique furniture and paintings, including a portrait by Sir Joshuah Reynolds of King George III and portraits of other British monarchs. It is sometimes possible to take tea with the Governor General at King's House as a guest of the 'Meet the People' programme run by the Jamaica Tourist Board; contact the JTB for details. Open 09:00–17:00 Mon–Sat (www.kingshouse.gov.jm).

Built in the 1960s as the premier's official residence, **Jamaica House** stands amid equally attractively landscaped grounds but is a rather less striking building. Jamaica House is not open to visitors.

UNIVERSITY OF THE WEST INDIES

The **Kingston Campus** of the University of the West Indies, at **Mona**, is one of UWI's three campuses (the others are in Barbados and Trinidad) serving the 14 independent English-speaking nations of the Caribbean. The adjoining **University Hospital of the West Indies** is the Caribbean's premier teaching hospital.

Bob Marley Museum ★★★

No tour of the city is complete without a visit to the museum at 56 Hope Road dedicated to Kingston's most famous son. Bob Marley's home and the studio of his **Tuff Gong** record label are now a museum tracing his career from ghetto childhood to international megastar. High points of the one-hour guided tour include a look at Marley's platinum and gold discs,

▼ Below: The Bob Marley Museum is the city's most popular attraction.

Rastafarian religious trappings, and the tree under which he liked to sit and smoke huge quantities of ganja (legend has it that the Marley household got through up to a pound of quality weed daily). There is also a 20-minute video compilation of Marley's greatest hits and live performances. Open 09:30–16.00 Mon–Sat with tours every hour (www.bobmarley-foundation.com).

Hope Botanical Gardens

The **Hope Estate**, now the home of the largest botanical gardens in the Caribbean region, is among the oldest estates in Jamaica. It was founded by one of Oliver Cromwell's officers, **Major Richard Hope**, who came to the Caribbean with the Parliamentary army in 1655. The 200-acre (81ha) gardens, next to the Mona Campus of the **University of the West Indies**, were bought from the government by the Hope Estate in 1881 and declared Jamaica's Royal Botanical Gardens in 1953, on the coronation of Queen Elizabeth II and her visit that year to Jamaica. The once-grand gardens feature ornamental ponds, cactus garden, shrubberies and greenhouses but have lost their former glory. Open 09.00–17.30 daily.

PORT ROYAL

There is little left at Port Royal to indicate that it was in its heyday known as 'the wickedest city in the world'. In the 17th century, this harbour city situated at the western end of the narrow, snake-like Palisadoes Peninsula which protects Kingston Harbour from the surf of the Caribbean was a safe haven for the most feared buccaneers of the Spanish Main – including men such as **Edward 'Blackbeard' Teach** (who ended his days on the executioner's gibbet) and **Henry Morgan** (who made good, was knighted by the Crown and became a Governor General of Jamaica). It was clearly not a place for honest, law-abiding folk and, when the earthquake of 7 June 1692 swept most of Port Royal into the sea, there were plenty who were ready to see the catastrophe as divine judgment on the wicked ways of its inhabitants.

▲ *Above: Port Royal was once the base for a group of buccaneers who made their living from attacking Spanish and other ships in the Caribbean.*

The Waterfront *

Today, the waterfront is a quiet fishing port (except, of course, at weekends when it attracts flocks of day-trippers from Kingston) with a handful of surviving 17th-, 18th- and 19th-century buildings to remind visitors of its glory days. Fishing pirogues and drying fishing nets line the waterside at **Fisherman's Beach**, just off Port Royal High Street.

There are ambitious plans to recreate Port Royal in the historical spirit of its pirating past, with more museums, shops and restaurants echoing a buccaneer theme, and already its historic buildings, two small museums and a veritable archipelago of offshore coral islets (perfect for swimming and snorkelling) make it worth the trip from central Kingston.

The drive to Port Royal takes you past the bobbing masts of the **Royal Jamaica Yacht Club** flotilla at anchor midway along the peninsula, and the runways of **Norman Manley International Airport**. Alternatively – and considerably more entertaining – take the ferry from Kingston's Pier 2, which leaves every two hours between 06:00 and 18:30.

SIR HENRY MORGAN

Henry Morgan (1635–1688) is one of the Caribbean's wildest success stories. Born in **Wales**, he came to the Caribbean as a bondsman in the early 1650s. At the end of his contract, he joined the **buccaneers** of Jamaica, quickly becoming one of their leaders in the bloody plundering of Spanish ports throughout the Caribbean, culminating in the sack of **Panama**, the greatest city in the **Spanish Main**. He was knighted for his contribution to England's victories, and on the principle of 'set a thief to catch a thief' was made **Governor of Jamaica**, where he lived, prospered, and eventually died in 1688.

▲ Above: Tilted on its foundation by an earthquake in 1907, the Giddy House previously served as an artillery store.

Fort Charles Maritime Museum **

After the earthquake of 1692, Port Royal was rebuilt and became the main Caribbean base of the **Royal Navy** for two centuries. The strongest of its defences was **Fort Charles**, established by Cromwell's troops when they occupied Jamaica in 1655 and strengthened in later years to become a formidable obstacle to would-be attackers. More than 100 massive cast-iron cannon bristle from the battlements of this solid red brick fortress, built to guard the approaches to the harbour from invasion by the French. In its heyday, these defences were augmented by a sea-water moat, but the whitewashed garrison buildings and flagstoned parade square are much as they must have been in Nelson's time.

Within the walls is also the little **Maritime Museum**, which has a collection of finely detailed ship models and a miscellany of maritime memorabilia from the days of sail. Open 09:00–17:00 Mon–Fri, 09:00–16:00 Sat.

Giddy House *

About 100 yards (91m) south of the fort, the small brick building half buried in the shingle of the nearby beach is known as the Giddy House, for obvious reasons. Tilted at a crazy angle, it was a victim not of the first Port Royal earthquake but of the 1907 earthquake, which clearly rocked it to its foundations. The plaque above the arched doorway reveals that it served as the **Royal Artillery Store**, built in 1888 during the reign of Queen Victoria. A large muzzle-loading cannon, tipped from its mounting on the massive brick emplacement next to the Giddy House, was another victim of the 1907 tremors, but beside it several more titanic 19th-century guns still point out to sea from the Victoria and Albert gun batteries.

NELSON'S QUARTERDECK

Among the commanders of **Fort Charles** was **Horatio Nelson**. He was only 20 when he was given command of the garrison in 1779, beginning the glorious career which was to lead to the birth of a legend. A plaque within the walls commemorates him, and the observation platform looking out to sea from the fortifications – where the young commander is said to have kept watch for the enemy's sails – is still known as Nelson's Quarterdeck, while the square in front of the fort is now named **Nelson Square**.

Archaeological and Historical Museum ★★

The small Archaeological and Historical Museum on Broad Street contains a collection of relics of old Port Royal, brought up from the sea bottom by fishermen's nets, dredged up by treasure seekers or discovered by scuba divers. Tales of pirate wealth keep people looking for fabled treasure swept into the sea by the earthquake three centuries ago. Though no great hoard of pieces of eight has ever been found, the museum has benefited from the continuing search, and boasts an interesting assortment of bits and pieces saved from the ocean bed. The museum occupies one of the rooms of the old **Naval Hospital,** a long building of cast iron construction which, though battered, has resisted several earthquakes. It was built in 1819 and overlooks Port Royal harbour. Open 09:00–16:00 weekdays, 10:00–17:00 weekends.

Old Gaol ★

The Old Gaol on New Street is one of Port Royal's oldest buildings. It survived the 1692 earthquake and must have housed some notorious evil-doers in its time, but today it shows little signs of its grim past and houses a selection of souvenir and craft shops. Open 09:00–17:00 Monday–Saturday.

PIRATEERS

Many saw the destruction of **Port Royal** in 1692 as a judgement on the wicked ways of its inhabitants. Although its days as a pirate capital were curtailed, piracy continued and, despite the best efforts of the Royal Navy, pirates such as **Edward 'Blackbeard' Teach**, **Nicholas Brown** and **'Calico Jack' Rackham** continued to plague Jamaican waters well into the 18th century.

▼ Below: Over 100 giant cast-iron cannon line the battlements of historic Fort Charles.

▲ *Above: Morgan's Harbour Hotel is the base for excursions to cays off the Palisadoes Peninsula.*

Lime Cay ★★

As your plane made its descent into Norman Manley airport you may have spotted a scattering of a dozen coral cays lying offshore from Port Royal, in the open water south of the **Palisadoes Peninsula**. These miniature islands have brilliant white coral-sand beaches and warm shallow water, and are perfect havens for swimming, snorkelling and sunbathing. They can become rather busy at weekends, when they attract Kingstonians seeking a break from the city streets, but are much less crowded during the week. The **Morgan's Harbour Hotel**, overlooking the harbour a few hundred metres from the centre of Port Royal, operates boat trips to **Lime Cay**, the biggest of these islands and, on request, to its smaller neighbours.

ST ANDREW PARISH

The parish of St Andrew forms the hinterland of Kingston, with splendid scenery on the slopes of the **Blue Mountains** which, in turn, offer magnificent views of both Kingston and its picturesque coast. Only one proper road crosses the Blue Mountains – the B1, which runs from Kingston, via **Castleton**, to Buff Bay on the north coast. In the northeast of the parish there are a number of sights worth seeing on a day trip from the capital.

Castleton Botanical Gardens ★★

Gigantic tree ferns reminiscent of *Jurassic Park*, more than 30 different kinds of palm tree, azaleas and dozens of other brilliant tropical flowering plants are highlights of this delightful garden, 20 miles (32km) north of Kingston on route A3. Founded in 1862, Castleton boasts an enormous array of flora, with more than 1000 different types of flowers and plant. Open 07:00–18:00 daily.

FRUITS OF JAMAICA

Delicious **coconut** and **pineapple** are on every buffet table and you'll meet plenty of beach vendors happy to slice the top from a green drinking coconut with a few deft strokes. Less familiar fruit include the **star apple**, a green or purple fruit with sweet white pulp which is served with grapefruit or orange, and the **sweetsop**, a smaller, sweeter cousin of the **soursop** with green skin and sweet pulp.

Newcastle Fort *

The grounds of the **Jamaica Defence Force** training camp, 12 miles (19km) north of Kingston on route B1, were originally a British colonial garrison, and are now open to visitors. The crests of the Jamaican regiments – both past and present – adorn the walls of the parade ground and there are fine mountain views. Open 08:00–17:00 daily (www.jdfmil.org).

Hollywell Forest Park

Situated on the B1, some 3 miles (5km) north of Newcastle, the woodlands of Hollywell remain a delight for both birdwatchers and walkers, with extensive hilltop views of Kingston. Hollywell was hit hard by Hurricane Gilbert in 1988, but many new trees have been planted and its forests are well on the way to recovery. Open 09:00–17:00 daily.

Cinchona Botanical Gardens **

Cinchona, perched high on the **Grand Ridge** of the Blue Mountains, 22 miles (35km) northeast of Kingston, is a colourful estate of landscaped gardens planted with exotic flowering trees and shrubs. Its original purpose, when set up in 1868, was to grow cinchona, the tree from which the anti-malarial drug quinine is extracted, and Assam tea. Neither crop was successful, and Cinchona became an ornamental garden instead. Open daily.

HEALING HERBS

Jamaicans have always placed great faith in natural herbal cures for ailments and – especially in rural Jamaica, where modern health care is out of the reach of many – numerous herbal cures are still in use. **Coconut water** is said to be good for the kidneys, and **fever grass tea** is drunk to alleviate aches and fever. Moving on from tradition to hard pharmacology, pioneering work by Jamaican biochemist Dr Henry Lowe, holds out hope for new drugs against cancer and HIV using substances synthesised from a common Jamaican plant, ball moss (*Tillandsia recurvata*).

◀ *Left: Over 1000 different types of flowers and plants may be found at thriving Castleton Botanical Gardens north of Kingston, founded in 1862.*

GANJA

Unless you look unbelievably straight, at some point during your stay you will be offered a taste of ganja (*cannabis indica*).
Rastafarians regard it as a sacramental herb. Dope contributes millions to Jamaica's illicit economy. What you are offered will certainly be described as **'sensimilla'** – the strongest kind – but is more likely to be **'bush'** – the commonest and cheapest. Ganja is no more harmful than other drugs such as tobacco and alcohol, and in Jamaica even policemen have been known to light up. However, possession is illegal, with potentially heavy penalties, and dogs trained to detect it will sniff your luggage as you leave Jamaica and on arrival back in the USA or UK.

BLUE MOUNTAINS

Peaking at altitudes of more than 7000ft (2200m) above sea level, the sierras of the **Blue Mountains** and the adjoining **John Crow Mountains** are visible from points all over the north, south and east coasts. Shrouded in mists the colour of cigar smoke, it's easy to see how the Blue Mountains got their name – though at close quarters their slopes are verdant and in many places cloaked in near-virgin forest. So far above the sea, the climate of the Blue Mountains is distinctly cooler than that of the coast, with more than 300 inches (7610mm) annual rainfall, and is ideal for growing coffee, bananas and another less reputable crop – ganja. The Grand Ridge of the Blue Mountains is almost 30 miles long and some 12 miles (20km) wide. Running diagonally across the island from northwest to southeast, merging at its eastern end with the John Crow range – which, in turn, runs parallel to the east coast of the island – the Grand Ridge is dominated by five summits: **John Crow**, at 5750ft (1762m); **Sir Johns**, at 6332ft (1930m); **Mossman's Peak**, at 6703ft (2043m); **High Peak**, at 6812ft (2076m); and **Blue Mountain Peak**, at 7402ft (2256m), the highest point in Jamaica. For the more energetic and adventurous, several tour companies organise trekking into the **Blue Mountains–John Crow National Park**, which occupies almost 200,000 acres (89,000ha) around the Blue Mountain Peak.

▶ Right: *Coffee cultivated in the verdant Blue Mountain range is generally exported for sale abroad, where it manages to command high prices in the frequently volatile international coffee market.*

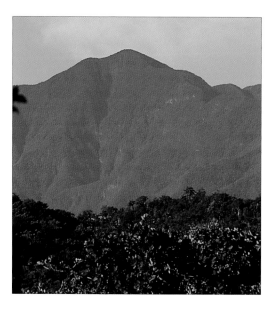

◄ *Left: The aptly named Blue Mountain Peak, seen from the north, is Jamaica's highest peak at 7402ft (2256m), with a climate that is distinctly cooler than on the coast.*

Blue Mountain Peak ★★★

The walk to the top of Blue Mountain Peak is rather a tough one, but the rewards along the way include the varied and colourful birdlife, flowers, plants and butterflies of the mountains – and some of the most magnificent views in Jamaica. Most treks start from **Mavis Bank**, a small settlement at the end of the road from Kingston via **Gordon Town** (about an hour's drive). The ascent takes at least four hours, so if you want to be on the peak in time for the magnificent sunrise you have to hit the trail by 02.00. The trail is steep and strenuous at the start, but the going gets a little easier as you climb higher. From the peak, the view is of tangled green jungle sloping down into blue mists, with the Caribbean sparkling in the distance beyond the **Kingston Plains** and the urban sprawl of the capital city far below. Any reasonably fit person should be able to complete the walk, which requires no technical skill, and if you can spare a couple of days from your sightseeing schedule it is very well worth doing.

RUM

Made from the treacly **molasses** extracted from sugar cane, rum in a dozen different guises has been Jamaica's favourite tipple since the days of the buccaneers. The most popular brands are **Wray**, **Sangster** and **Appleton**, all of which produce white rum – most often used in cocktails and punches – as well as gold rum aged in oak casks. Strongest of all is **overproof rum**. With an alcohol content of up to 80% – and a kick like a bucking bronco! – it should be drunk with extreme caution.

BEST TIMES TO VISIT

Jamaica's climate is moderate year-round, but the heat and humidity from May to November, along with seasonal rains, make it officially off-season.

GETTING THERE

Norman Manley International Airport is on the Palisadoes Peninsula, 10 miles (16km) and 30 minutes from downtown Kingston. Touts offer rides into town, but most of the main hotels operate shuttles.

GETTING AROUND

Car hire: Drivers must be over 21 and have British, EU, US or Canadian licence. Car hire is expensive and is not recommended within Kingston. **Avis** (tel: 926 8021); **Budget** (tel: 759 1793 or 759 1353. Four-wheel-drive is essential for Blue Mountain trips.

Taxis: Kingston's best travel option, but agree on the fare before boarding. Licensed cabs have red **Public Passenger Vehicle** (PPV) licence plates.

Buses: Crowded and uncomfortable – and a real risk from pickpockets and bagsnatchers.

Tourist coaches: Jamaican Union of Travellers Associations (JUTA), tel: 926 1537, runs tourist taxis (comfortable but not cheap) and shuttles between resorts (www.jutatoursjamaica.com).

WHERE TO STAY

New Kingston Area

LUXURY

Spanish Court Hotel, 1 St Lucia Ave, tel: 926 0000, www.spanishcourthotel.com New and very stylish hotel with 109 rooms and suites, all chicly decorated. Suites have frills such as wide-screen plasma TV and iPod dock, there is free Wi-Fi access throughout the hotel, and there's a very cool rooftop pool and bar terrace.

Jamaica Pegasus Hotel, 81 Knutsford Blvd, Kingston 5, tel: 926 3690, www.jamaicapegasus.com Four-star in financial district, managed by international chain. Tennis court, pool, restaurants, bars, nightly entertainment and facilities for the handicapped.

MID-RANGE

Altamont Court Hotel, 1–3 Altamont Terrace, Kingston 5, tel: 929 4497, www.altamontcourt.com Central, family owned; pool.

Courtleigh Hotel, 85 Knutsford Blvd, Kingston 5, tel: 936 3570, www.courtleigh.com 127 rooms and suites; swimming pool; Wi-Fi.

Indies Hotel, 5 Holborn Road, Kingston 10, tel: 926 2952, www.indieshotel.com Small but stylish family hotel in the centre of New Kingston, with 15 air-conditioned rooms either side of a pretty garden courtyard.

Knutsford Court Hotel, 16 Chelsea Ave, Kingston 10, tel: 929 1000, www.knutsfordcourt.com Offers excellent value and good facilities in the centre of town.

Terra Nova Hotel, 17 Waterloo Road, Kingston 10, tel: 926 2211, www.terranovajamaica.com Secluded, elegant; 21 rooms. Own pool, restaurants, bar.

Mayfair Hotel, PO Box 163, Kingston 10, tel: 929 1610, fax: 929 7441. Eight villas with garden. Pool, restaurant, bar.

BUDGET

Sunset Inn, 1A Altamont Cres, tel: 929 7383 www.sunsetinn-ja.com Pleasant small hotel with air-conditioned rooms and self-contained studio suites with kitchenettes.

Port Royal Area

LUXURY

Morgan's Harbour Hotel, Port Royal, tel: 967 8030, www.morgansharbour.com Near city, seafront restaurant, marina, water sports.

Blue Mountains

LUXURY

Strawberry Hill, Irish Town, tel: 944 8400, www.strawberryhillresort.com Remote, self-contained; 12 villas halfway up Blue Mountains. Airy rooms. Airport shuttle and helicopter available for fee.

WHERE TO EAT

Kingston has everything from roadside shacks to hotel restaurants, but none reach gourmet status. On a budget, head for a 'jerk centre'.

Central Kingston

LUXURY

Columbus Restaurant, Jamaica Pegasus Hotel, 81 Knutsford Boulevard, tel: 926 2690. Fine Italian dining in the lobby level of the Jamaica Pegasus Hotel.

Norma's on the Terrace, Devon House, 26 Hope Rd, Kingston 8, tel: 968 5488, fax: 925 5757. Superb, innovative Jamaican cuisine in the grounds of Devon House.

La Fresca Bar and Grill, Terra Nova Hotel, 17 Waterloo Road, tel: 926 9334. Elegant outdoor dining on the Terra Nova's verandah. Signature dishes include fish escoveitch, conch fritters, lobster and peppered shrimp.

MID-RANGE

Country Style Restaurant, 14 Main St, Stony Hill, St Andrew, tel: 942 2506, www.country stylerestaurantjamaica.com Good, traditional Jamaican dishes from rice and peas to callaloo, jerk pork, fish and chicken.

Guilt Trip, 20 Barbican Road, tel: 977 5130. Renowned for its outstanding sweet pastries and other island dishes.

Hot Pot, 2 Altamont Terrace, tel: 929 3906. Traditional dishes such as curry goat, 'run down', jerk pork.

Redbones Blues Café, 21 Braemar Ave, tel: 978 8262. Great Caribbean-Cajun food, live music in the evenings, poetry readings – all in an old Kingston townhouse with a walled garden.

Casson's Restaurant and Bar, 1D Braemar Ave, tel: 927 7114. Casual dining, pub food, cold beer and cocktails in the heart of the New Kingston business district.

BUDGET

Dragon City, 17 Northside Plaza, Liguanea, tel: 927 0939. Authentic and very affordable Chinese food, open for lunch and dinner.

Mingles Pub, 85 Knutsford Blvd, tel: 929 9000. Snacks, light meals with a Caribbean and South American flavour, live music and karaoke nights.

Peppers Night Club, 31 Upper Waterloo Road, tel: 969 2421. Excellent jerk food and international dishes (grills, pasta, pizza, seafood) at this lively open air bar and grill.

Miss May's, Hellshire Beach. Kingstonians who know where to find the freshest seafood and the best *escoveitch* head for this shack restaurant on the beach just outside town.

Port Royal

LUXURY

Sir Henry's, Morgan's Harbour Hotel, Port Royal, tel: 924 8464. Best view of harbour; fresh seafood.

TOURS AND EXCURSIONS

Touring Society of Jamaica, tel: 944 8400. Sightseeing and birding tours in and around Kingston and Jamaica.

Sun Venture, tel: 960 6685, www.sunventure.com Hikes, camping trips and birding in the Blue Mountains and the Cockpit Country.

Galaxy Leisure and Tours, tel: 925 4176, www.galaxy leisuretours.com Tours of historic Kingston and Port Royal, the Blue Mountains and around the island.

Forres Park Nature Retreat and Adventure Tours, Mavis Bank, tel: 927 8275. Four wheel drive, mountain bike or hiking tours in the Blue Mountains, with accommodation in a comfortable 14-room mountain chalet.

Great Vacations, tel: 927 5948, www.greatvac.com Excursions and tours all round the island, airport and hotel transfers and weddings; offices in Kingston, Ocho Rios and Montego Bay.

Jamaica Tourist Board (HO), 64 Knutsford Blvd, tel: 929 9200, www.visitjamaica.com

KINGSTON	J	F	M	A	M	J	J	A	S	O	N	D
AVERAGE TEMP. °C	30	30	30	32	32	33	33	33	33	32	32	32
AVERAGE TEMP. °F	86	86	86	90	90	92	92	92	92	90	90	90
RAINFALL mm	25	25	25	75	100	75	50	100	150	175	150	25
RAINFALL ins.	1	1	1	3	4	3	2	4	6	7	6	1
DAYS OF RAINFALL	1	1	1	6	7	6	5	10	12	14	12	1

3
Portland and St Thomas

Rugged mountainscapes, thick tropical rainforests, coffee plantations, sea cliffs and the exclusive hideaways of the rich and famous are some of the characteristics of Jamaica's two easternmost parishes. Together with St Andrew (the parish surrounding Kingston), **Portland** and **St Thomas** make up the county of **Surrey**. The latter two parishes are divided by the **Grand Ridge** of the Blue Mountains. To the east, beyond the Blue Mountain range, the **John Crow Mountains** rise steeply, cutting the Portland hinterland off from the sea. Like the Cockpit Country of Trelawny parish in the northwest of the island, the hill country of Portland and St Thomas is one of the most inaccessible and sparsely inhabited parts of the island, and there are no main roads through the heart of this territory. In centuries long past, its dripping virgin forest and thick undergrowth provided a refuge for fierce – and fearless – bands of proud Maroon warriors, whose descendants still dwell in remote mountain villages.

The coasts of Portland and St Thomas, in contrast with the region's rugged interior, hide some of Jamaica's most exclusive, elegant and sophisticated resorts. On the north coast lies Port Antonio, the birthplace of tourism in Jamaica and still a favoured retreat. From here back-to-nature sightseeing excursions run into the interior, exploring the region's caves, waterfalls and deep jungle gorges, or experiencing the excitement of river rafting.

CARIBBEAN SEA

DON'T MISS

*** Port Antonio: beautiful scenery, islands and fine beaches.
*** Blue Hole: spectacular lagoon of vivid turquoise water.
*** Rio Grande: bamboo rafting through stands of giant bamboo.
*** Blue Mountain Peak: fantastic views from the highest summit in Jamaica.
** Reach Falls: beautiful series of cascades, one of the island's most striking sights.

◄ *Opposite: Port Antonio's coastline is home to exclusive villas and resorts.*

49

▲ Above: The thrilling International Blue Marlin Tournament takes place off the shores of Port Antonio each October.

PORT ANTONIO

Turquoise waters dotted with small jungle-like islands, clear winding rivers, green hillsides, and beaches dotted with colourful fishing pirogues ... the stunning beauty of the Port Antonio area has lured the bold and the beautiful since Errol Flynn's day and before. It is hard to believe today, looking at its quintessentially sleepy quaysides and streets, that this was where Jamaican tourism was born. Built around a natural harbour, the resorts and villas around this little port, some 70 miles (130km) northeast of Kingston, are among Jamaica's most exclusive and expensive. They still attract a clientele of Hollywood stars and minor Eurotrash, and the surrounding area has been a favourite location for movie producers since the 1960s. With the silhouetted peaks of the Blue Mountains as a backdrop, this is undoubtedly one of the island's most unspoilt resort areas, though the town itself has seen better days and has little in the way of sightseeing attractions.

As its name implies, Port Antonio was named by the first Spanish settlers, who could hardly ignore such a haven, and they dubbed it Puerto Anton. But the hinterland was rugged and extremely ill suited to cultivation, and other, more easily settled parts of the island attracted the attention of the Spaniards and their British successors. The first proper settlement at Port Antonio was in the early 18th century, but it remained a backwater fishing harbour until the late 19th century, when the advent of refrigerated cargo vessels brought about a Caribbean banana boom. The hillsides inland proved ideal for banana planting, and Port Antonio entered a golden age of prosperity. Banana shippers had the bright idea of bringing visitors to Jamaica from US ports to escape the chilly northern winter, and the first wealthy tourists set the tone for generations to come.

Fort George *

Port Antonio consists of two bays, **West Harbour** and **East Harbour**, which are divided by the **Titchfield Peninsula**. Titchfield School, at the tip of this peninsula, occupies the site of **Fort George**, which was built in 1729 to defend the harbours. A handful of cannon can be seen in the school grounds, surrounded by the 10ft (3m) thick walls of the original fort.

Navy Island ***

Australian-born film star **Errol Flynn** put Navy Island on the map quite by chance – his yacht was forced to take shelter in Port Antonio harbour during a hurricane and he liked the place so much that he bought this small island just off Titchfield Point to use as his private hideaway. Currently closed for renovation (no re-opening date has been set) and it is not open to non-residents.

▼ Below: Beautiful Navy Island is accessible only by water taxi.

BLUE HOLES

Most of Jamaica's geology is **limestone**, and millennia of tropical rains have carved out extensive **cave systems** in the Jamaican hills, many of them still to be explored. The limestone rock has also been hollowed out by rain and wave action into deep waterfilled 'blue holes' connecting to the sea, some of which offer exciting cave-diving adventures, such as **God's Well**, a 160ft (50m) sinkhole on the **Long Bay** coast.

Athenry Gardens and Nonsuch Caves ★★

About 2 miles (5km) southeast of Port Antonio, and 1000ft (330m) above sea level, this former coconut plantation embraces 185 acres (34ha) of rainforest and a profusion of spectacular tropical plants. The plantation affords fine views of the coast and the John Crow Mountains.

About a mile from Athenry, though still within the plantation grounds, are nine interconnected caves, known as the **Nonsuch Caves**. The caves contain strange limestone and volcanic formations, as well as fossils, and are the haunt of hundreds of tiny bats. Currently closed, and no reopening date has been set.

San San Beach ★★★

Port Antonio's best beach – the one that attracts the stars – is 5 miles (8km) east of town at San San, where a dazzling crescent of powdery coral sand is backed by three luxury hotels and a nine-hole golf course. The beach is private, and there is an entry charge for those not lucky enough to be staying at one of the luxury resorts there. Open 10:00–22:00 daily.

Blue Hole (Blue Lagoon) ★★★

A few hundred metres east of San San Beach, the Blue Hole, also called the **Blue Lagoon**, is at least 200ft (60m) deep – underwater explorer Jacques Cousteau is said to have dived to at least that depth and found no bottom. The 'hole' is a limestone sink and its almost luminous turquoise waters are ringed by vivid green foliage. It has been used as a location for many movies including the 1980 Brooke Shields teen film *Blue Lagoon*. Floodlit at night, the lagoon is a sight more memorable than any of the films which have been shot there, and you can only envy those who can afford the luxury of a private villa on its shores. Open 10:00–22:00 daily.

▶ *Opposite: Rafting on the Rio Grande is a popular activity and attracts company on the river.*
▼ *Below: The Blue Hole is surprisingly deep, its water a remarkable shade of turquoise.*

WEST OF PORT ANTONIO
Rio Grande ★★★

The bamboo rafts which are now used to carry tourists down Jamaica's longest river, were originally used by banana planters to ferry their crop to the coast at St Margaret's Bay, about 5 miles (8km) west of Port Antonio. Once again, it was the actor Errol Flynn who turned the Rio Grande into a vacation experience, taking guests staying at his Navy Island home on trips down the river. Today, the raft ride – on long, slender bamboo craft poled by singing gondoliers – takes about three hours and the

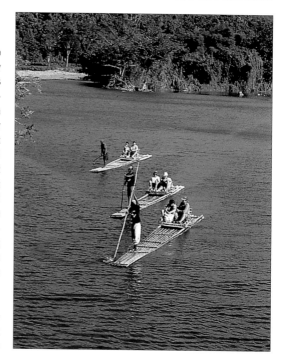

route extends through lush jungle scenery. Visitors are able to take a raft trip day or night – it is especially popular on romantic moonlit nights. Rio Grande rafting is, however, one of Jamaica's most highly commercialised holiday activities, and it can seem that virtually every foot of the river bank has been staked out by somebody who is trying to sell you something. Open 09:00–15:30 daily.

Sommerset Falls ★

At Sommerset Falls, 12 miles (20km) west of Port Antonio, the **Daniels River** forms a series of pools and cataracts beneath a canopy of bamboos, ferns and wild bananas. Although the falls themselves are actually quite tame, visitors may choose to swim in a nearby chasm. Open 09:00–17:00.

SALTFISH AND ACKEE

It's hard to believe that something which so closely resembles scrambled egg grows on a tree, but **ackee**, the favourite Jamaican breakfast dish, comes from the pod-like fruits of a tree imported to the island from West Africa. Ackee is usually served with **salt cod**, originally imported from Newfoundland as a cheap food for slaves and now regarded as a luxury to be eaten on special occasions. You will find saltfish and ackee on most resort breakfast buffets.

MOORE TOWN

Moore Town, a clutch of simple wooden homes and buildings only 10 miles (16km) south of Port Antonio, is a step back on the road to ancestral Africa. It is the capital of the proud **Windward Maroons**, one of two communities created in the 18th and 19th centuries by escapees from slavery. Moore Town and the region around it, under a treaty signed between the British and the Maroons in 1739, have some degree of self-government, with day-to-day affairs administered by a Maroon council of 24 headed by a hereditary 'Colonel'. Other Maroon communities in the neighbourhood include **Comfort Castle**, **Seaman's Valley** and **Ginger Town**, but the Maroon remain proudly aloof from tourism and to make the most of a trip to their mountains it is advisable to contact the Maroon Council, through the Jamaica Tourist Board, in order to arrange a guided visit.

Sam Sharpe Museum *

The small Sam Sharpe Museum located on Main Street commemorates one of Jamaica's national heroes, the rebel leader Sam Sharpe, who inspired the **Christmas Rebellion** of 1831–2 which was to lead to the ending of the slave system in 1834. The museum also tells of the Maroons' unique dialect and way of life, which retain strong West African elements. Open 09:00–17:00 Monday–Friday.

Bump Grave *

Outside Moore Town's small school, situated just off Main Street, stands a plain stone column which is said to mark the final resting place of **Nanny**, the 17th-century chieftainess who governed over the Windward Maroons. The much-revered Nanny was declared a national heroine in 1975, when the monument was placed here. The site of Nanny Town, her capital, is said to be in the Blue Mountains high above Moore Town, but it was completely destroyed in 1734 and no trace remains.

MAROONS

The Maroons – descended from runaway **Spanish slaves** and **Coromantee warriors** from the **Gold Coast** (now Ghana) who escaped in the **Clarendon** slave uprising of 1690 – are aptly named (from *cimarron*, Spanish for 'wild'). Their bush warfare and survival skills helped them maintain their freedom, and even after two wars against the British – the second ending in the deportation of 600 of them to Canada – they managed to keep control of their own affairs, under their own rulers, though they had to agree to return runaway slaves to white custody. Today, the Maroons are concentrated around **Moore Town**, in the mountains south of Port Antonio, and **Maroon Town**, in the Cockpit Country.

EAST COAST
Long Bay *

Around 12 miles (20km) east of Port Antonio, Long Bay has two of Jamaica's most spectacular beaches. You may at first be surprised at the lack of tourism development here, since the location seems ideal, but the exposed crescent bays are vulnerable to high seas in the hurricane season – and even in calmer weather there is a fierce undertow – which makes swimming dangerous and has deterred even daring fishermen from settling here.

Manchioneal *

Manchioneal is the only good anchorage on this exposed coast, and a small fishing hamlet has grown up around its natural harbour. The deep blue bay and the colourful wooden dugout canoes hauled up on Manchioneal's narrow beach make it a perfect photo opportunity, but there is little to see or do other than to relax and take in the sunshine and the majestic setting.

Reach Falls **

Reach Falls, about 20 miles (32km) southeast of Port Antonio, is one of the island's most spectacular sights, rivalling the more famous Dunn's River Falls near Ocho Rios. The falls cascade in four cataracts, the tallest of which is some 40ft (13m) high, and each terminates in a deep green pool (although swimming is allowed, strong under-currents make it rather dangerous). A gaggle of dreadlocked higglers sell the usual array of carvings and ornaments. Open daily, daylight hours.

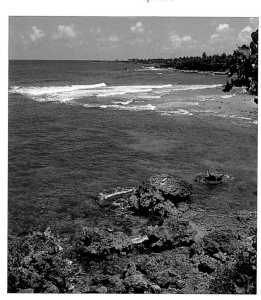

▼ *Below: Long Bay's exposed position has deterred development.*

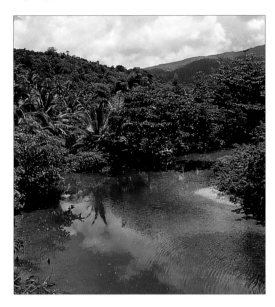

BATH

Rather aptly named after the renowned English spa, Bath has been favoured for its natural hot springs ever since 1699. This small town is clearly long past its Victorian heyday, when it attracted the very wealthiest of trendsetters on the island to bathe in its supposedly healing waters, but visitors are still welcome to emulate the early holiday-makers, and to unwind in the soothing waters of this picturesque district.

▲ Above: River waters near Bath are said to have medicinal properties.

FOREST FLAME

Jamaica wouldn't be the same without the blazing scarlet, orange and vermilion flowers of the 'Flame of the Forest' or **poinciana**. Native to Madagascar, its spreading boughs shade many island roads and homes. The **flame tree** flowers for much of the year, but between February and April its flowers and foliage give way to bare branches and gigantic seed pods. Up to 20 inches (50cm) long, these make natural rattles for children and maracas for reggae and calypso musicians.

Bath Fountain Hotel *

The Bath Fountain Hotel is 2 miles (3km) north of town and its natural hot spring baths, open to visitors, are held to cure all manner of ills. A half-hour wallow will certainly ease muscular aches and pains. The waters of the mineral springs have high concentrations of sulphur and calcium, and emerge from a source close to the rather aptly named **Sulphur River** at temperatures of around 50–55°C (115–128°F). Open daily (tel: 703 4345, e-mail: bathmineralspahotelja@yahoo.com).

Botanical Gardens *

When not steaming themselves in the thermal baths, Victorian visitors strolled in the botanical gardens, founded in 1779 to cultivate exotic plants imported to Jamaica by seafarers such as **Captain William Bligh** of HMS *Bounty*, who brought the breadfruit to the island. The colourful gardens, adjoining the small church in the centre of Bath, are very photogenic and still worth a short visit. Open daily 05:30–18:00 (www.jnht.com).

ST THOMAS COAST
Morant Point Lighthouse *
The red-and-white striped lighthouse which marks Jamaica's southeastern extremity seems to lean at a precarious angle, like the Leaning Tower of Pisa, and looks set to eventually topple into the Caribbean. The cast-iron tower was made in London and the pre-fabricated segments bolted together and erected at Morant Point in 1841. If the keeper is in, you may be able to persuade him to take you to the open gallery at the top, from which there are panoramic views of the coast and out to sea. The lighthouse is open to visitors at varying times, and only in daylight hours.

Port Morant *
Like Port Antonio, Port Morant – a fine natural harbour on the St Thomas south coast, some 50 miles (80km) east of Kingston – flourished when the banana industry took off but later lost some of it lustre. However, unlike Port Antonio it has never attracted flocks of rich northern holiday-makers. Port Morant bay has small beaches at **Lyssons**, on the west side, and **Roselle**, on the east, which are popular with local people at weekends.

Morant Bay *
Morant Bay, now a quiet town on the south coast where the road from Bath meets the round-the-island highway, some 40 miles (64km) east of Kingston, was the scene of bloody confrontation between Jamaica's white ruling class and emancipated, but still oppressed, black Jamaicans. The **Morant Bay Rebellion** of 1865, led by preacher **Paul Bogle**, left 28 dead. In reprisal, the authorities hanged Bogle, legislator **George William Gordon**, and 430 accused rebels. Thousands more were savagely flogged. But this barbaric response backfired on the plantocracy,

Two of Jamaica's parrot species are found nowhere else in the world and are considered endangered – due largely to the destruction of their habitat and the poaching of eggs and fledglings for the pet trade. The **yellow-billed parrot** (*Amazona collaria*) is one of Jamaica's loveliest birds, around 11 inches (28cm) in size with primrose-yellow beak, rose-pink throat and green back and wings, with turquoise highlights on the head, tail and wings. The even rarer **black-billed parrot** (*Amazona agilis*) is 10 inches (25cm) in size, with charcoal-grey beak and eyes and green plumage.

▼ Below: Exotic plants such as this ginger lily fare well in Jamaica's climate.

THE MONGOOSE

The mongoose was introduced from **India** to deal with cane rats and snakes infesting sugar cane. Jamaica is now almost snake-free – with its surviving serpents now endangered. The mongoose has also wiped out several native bird species and continues to endanger others, including poultry, making it a far greater pest than the snakes ever were.

and an investigation into the affair by a British Royal Commission led to the island being declared a Crown Colony, with the planters losing much of their power to oppress black Jamaicans.

The unusually powerful **Paul Bogle Monument**, a memorial to the leader of the uprising, sculpted by Edna Manley, stands in Morant Bay's town square. Nearby is **Morant Bay Fort**, which was built in 1773. The fort encloses a park commemorating those executed after the 1865 violence, and 79 skeletons found interred behind the walls of the fort during digging in 1965 were buried here in a common grave. Old iron cannon, dating from the 19th century, still stand on the battlements.

Yallahs

Midway between Morant Bay and Kingston, on the A4 coastal highway, Yallahs is little more than a truck-stop, surrounded by countryside which is almost desert-like by Jamaican standards, as it lies in the rain-shadow of the Blue Mountains. Yallahs has two minor attractions for those with a special interest in history or ornithology.

▼ Below: Morant Bay is a peaceful town on the south coast, no longer touched by the events of its somewhat turbulent past.

Yallah Ponds *

On the coast a few hundred metres east of Yallahs village begins a narrow natural breakwater, formed by silt deposited by the broad, shallow **Yallahs River**. This stretches for almost 5 miles (8km) and encloses a vast, shallow brine lagoon which is a haven for flocks of seabirds that feed on the huge shoals of brine shrimp and other plankton breeding in the salty water.

Kach Mansong Monument *

Kach Mansong, also called **Three Fingered Jack**, was an escaped slave who took to a life of banditry in the foothills of the Blue Mountains in the late 18th century. Regarded as a murderer by the British authorities, he was a Robin Hood figure to many enslaved Jamaicans and is commemorated by a monument erected by the Jamaican National Heritage Trust. The site of the monument, beside the road 6 miles (10km) west of Yallahs on the A4, is the spot where he was ambushed and killed in 1781 by Maroon trackers in the pay of the authorities.

THE FLAG

Jamaica's black, green and yellow national flag, run up for the first time on 6 August 1962, was inspired by both **Norman Manley**, leader of the People's National Party and one of the fathers of Jamaican independence, and by his great rival, **Alexander Bustamante**, the country's first prime minister. Proudly pro-British, Bustamante wanted a flag reminiscent of the Union Flag of Britain, while Manley believed the new banner should symbolise all the peoples of Jamaica. The result is a black, green and gold national flag incorporating a **St Andrew's Cross**. Its colours fly over official buildings and adorn Rasta hats and countless holiday T-shirts.

Best Times to Visit

Jamaica's climate is moderate year-round, but the heat and humidity May–November, along with seasonal rains, make it officially off-season.

Getting There

By Land: If you are travelling on a package tour, your tour company will provide minibus transfer from Kingston, the nearest airport, or from Ocho Rios. Public transport is thin on the ground, and the only realistic alternatives to organised tours are self-drive **cars** or **taxis**. Port Antonio is approximately 60 miles (100km) northeast of Kingston, and the steep, winding drive through the Blue Mountains takes three hours or more.

Getting Around

The only feasible way of travelling within Portland and St Thomas is by **taxi** or **hire car**: **Port Antonio Car Rentals**, 26 Harbour Street, Port Antonio, tel: 993 3624. **Buses** are too infrequent and irregular to be useful to the visitor. A coastal highway, the A4, runs all the way from the Portland/St Mary parish line in the north, through Port Antonio, Manchioneal, Morant Bay and Yallahs on the south coast to Kingston. The B1, a remarkable piece of road-building with many hairpin bends, cuts north through the Blue Mountains from Kingston to Buff Bay on the north coast, where it meets the A4. During the July–September rainy season, many of the unsurfaced roads in the region may become virtually impassable.

Where to Stay

Almost all of the accommodation in the Port Antonio area is at the luxury end of the range and is priced accordingly. However, there is virtually no accommodation available beyond the Port Antonio area.

Luxury

Blue Lagoon Villas, Fairy Hill, Port Antonio, tel: 978 6245, www.blue lagoonvillas.com Ultra luxurious, intimate villa resort right on the water's edge at Blue Lagoon. Each villa comes with its own full kitchen and sun deck with steps into the water, resident maid, cook and butler, and the price includes chauffeured transfers to and from the airport. Kayaks are available and there is free access to Blue Lagoon and Frenchman's Cove beaches.

Trident Castle, PO Box 119, Anchovy, Port Antonio, tel: 993 2602, fax: 993 2590, www.tridentcastle.com Luxury establishment, with 26 bedrooms furnished with colonial antiques, private balconies and verandas. Private beach, swiming pool, tennis courts, restaurant and two bars.

Jamaica Palace Hotel, PO Box 277, Williamsfield, Port Antonio, tel: 993 7720, www.jamaica-palacehotel. com Luxury hotel on the beach.

Goblin Hill Villas (San San), 11 East Avenue, Kingston 10, tel: 925 8108, www.goblinhillvillas.com Lush 12-acre (5ha) retreat on the exclusive San San Estate; 28 villas with breathtaking beach views.

Mid-range

Bonnie View Plantation Hotel, PO Box 82, Richmond Hill, Port Antonio, tel: 993 2752, fax: 993 2862. Small, charming hotel, 22 rooms on 25-acre (10ha) working plantation. Fine views of the sea and the mountains. Good base for riding and hiking excursions.

Hotel Mocking Bird Hill, PO Box 254, Port Antonio, tel: 993 7134, www.hotel mockingbirdhill.com 10 rooms, restaurant and bar five minutes' walk from the beach.

Fern Hill Club Hotel & Villa Resort, Mile Gully Road, PO Box 100, Port Antonio, tel: 993 7375, www.fernhill clubhotel.com All-inclusive, with 40 double/twin rooms, 16 with whirlpool spa; nightly entertainment, restaurant, two bars. Located on San San Beach.

WHERE TO EAT

Port Antonio

LUXURY

Mille Fleurs,
Hotel Mocking Bird Hill,
tel: 993 7134. À la carte
restaurant with a menu
stressing seafood in exotic
spice and fruit sauces,
served on a lush terrace
with great sunset views.

Blue Lagoon Restaurant,
Blue Lagoon, tel: 993 8491.
Magnificent location overlooking the splendid lagoon,
which is floodlit at night.
Fine dining and a good
range of cocktails.

MID-RANGE

**Bonnie View Plantation
Hotel,** PO Box 82,
Richmond Hill, Port Antonio.
Worth visiting as much for
the marvellous view from the
terrace as for the Caribbean
and international menu.

DeMontevin Lodge,
Titchfield Street, Port
Antonio, tel: 993 2604.
Jamaican cuisine in a
delightfully restored
18th-century building,
once the home of an
English admiral.

BUDGET

Boston Beach Jerk Centre,
Boston Bay (no tel). About
8 miles (12km) east of Port
Antonio, this establishment
is well worth visiting (as
the Jamaicans do) for
probably the best jerk pork,
chicken and fish in Jamaica.

The food sold from a line
of small beachside stalls,
each with its own speciality
on the menu. Look out for
piquant boiled shrimp and
junga, a locally caught
freshwater crayfish. The
best time to visit is during
the day.

Woody's Low Bridge Place,
Drapers, Port Antonio, tel:
993 7888. Great curries,
chicken, fish and outstanding
vegetarian dishes are served
at this colourful shack-
restaurant on the outskirts
of Port Antonio.

SHOPPING

Unlike Kingston, Ocho Rios,
and Montego Bay (all of
which have extensive shopping facilities catering to the
American cruise passengers
who tend to pass through),
Port Antonio has very few
worthwhile retail outlets and
no big shopping malls.

Musgrave Market, on West
Street, is a lively producer
market, busiest from
08:00–12:00 (especially on
Saturdays). **Port Antonio
Marina** has more than 30
stylish shops and boutiques,
and **Gallery Carriacou**, in the
Hotel Mocking Bird Hills, the
place to go for outstanding
and original work by
Jamaican artists.

Designer's Gallery, Jamaica
Palace Hotel, sells Jamaican
carvings, paintings and beach
clothing, all of which tend to
be highly priced.

TOURS AND EXCURSIONS

Crystal Springs, Buff Bay,
tel: 993 2609. Orchids and
tropical birds to be seen on
guided tour of former sugar-
cane plantation, now a
156-acre (63ha) ecotourism
attraction with picnic ground
and botanical garden.

Rio Grande Rafting, Rafter's
Rest, St Margaret's Bay, tel:
993 2778. Prepare yourself
for an 8-mile (13km) guided
raft trip takes between two
and four hours.

Riding: Bonnie View
Plantation Hotel, PO Box
82, Richmond Hill, Port
Antonio, tel: 993 2752,
fax: 448 5398. Organises
guided horse-riding and
hiking in the foothills
inland from Port Antonio.

Lady Godiva's Dive Shop,
Port Antonio Marina, tel:
428 3437, www.ladygdiver.
com Offers a range of deep-
and shallow-water dives at
some of Jamaica's most
outstanding dive sites.

USEFUL CONTACTS

Jamaica Tourist Board,
City Centre Plaza, PO Box
151, Port Antonio, tel: 993
3051, fax: 993 2117.

**Jamaica Union of
Travellers Association**,
Port Antonio Chapter,
17 Harbour Street, Port
Antonio, tel: 993 2684.
Taxis, airport and resort
transfers, and tours to all
the popular sightseeing
attractions of the region.

4
St Ann and St Mary

The parishes of St Ann and St Mary occupy the central third of Jamaica's north coast and its hinterland, with some splendid beaches and natural harbours backed by a coastal plain of sugar-cane fields rising gradually to rolling hills. The scenery here is pastoral rather than grand, with hills rising to only 2759ft (800m) at their highest point.

St Ann Parish can claim, in a sense, to be the heart of modern Jamaican history, for it was on this coast, where the appropriately named village of **Discovery Bay** now stands, that Christopher Columbus made his first landfall on the island, naming the spot **Rio Bueno**. The ruined foundations of **Sevilla la Nueva**, the first settlement founded by his conquistadors, may still be seen at **St Ann's Bay**, but the Spaniards soon moved their headquarters to **Villa de la Vega** (now Spanish Town) on the south coast, which had a much better anchorage. It was later from St Ann Parish that the last Spaniards fled Jamaica – from the shores of **Runaway Bay**, now a popular north coast resort – after being defeated by the British in 1658.

After the Spaniards came the British sugar planters, who left the fertile coastal plains patchworked with cane plantations. As sugar declined in importance, the north coast became a thriving centre for a new Jamaican boom industry – **tourism**. Among the first sun-seeking migrants to north shore resorts were wealthy expatriates such as English actor, playwright and musician Sir Noel Coward, and James Bond creator

CARIBBEAN SEA

Don't Miss

*** Ocho Rios: some of Jamaica's finest beaches and resorts.
*** Dunn's River Falls: the island's most famous waterfalls.
*** Green Grotto: explore deep limestone caverns on foot or by boat.
*** Firefly: Sir Noel Coward's lovely villa, with magnificent views.
** White River: rafting experience through tropical riverside scenery.
** Harmony Hall: fine wooden traditional residence with excellent art collection.

◄ *Opposite: Superb beaches line the coast of Jamaica.*

ADMIRAL NELSON

Horatio Nelson (1758–1805) joined the Royal Navy in 1770, spending much of the early part of his naval career in Jamaica and the Caribbean, where he was promoted to commander in 1778, returning in 1782–83 and again in 1784–87. Nelson is as well known for his defiance of orders, and physical disabilities – an eye lost at Calvi in 1794, and a right arm at Santa Cruz three years later – as for his victories in the French wars. He was made vice-admiral and created **Viscount Nelson** in 1801, and killed by a musket ball in the hour of his victory at **Trafalgar**.

Ian Fleming, both of whom had villas overlooking the sea. In their steps have followed millions of visitors, many of them pausing only briefly before their cruise ship takes them onward to new destinations, others staying longer to make the most of the north coast's many attractions.

OCHO RIOS AREA

The thriving resort centre of Ocho Rios, midway between Montego Bay and Port Antonio and almost the same distance from Kingston, has come a long way from its roots as a fishing village to become the main holiday centre and port of call for cruise ships on the north coast. With beaches on either side and plenty of sightseeing attractions nearby, Ocho Rios, known to locals as 'Ochi', is one of Jamaica's holiday favourites. The town's name means 'Eight Rivers' in Spanish, but visitors will look in vain for them. In fact, it is a corruption of *las chorreras*, Spanish for 'waterfalls' and is appropriate enough, as Jamaica's best-known scenic falls are just outside town, and smaller cascading streams are a feature of the coast east of Ocho Rios. The original village of Ocho Rios, now the downtown section of the resort with a multi-storey hotel and apart-

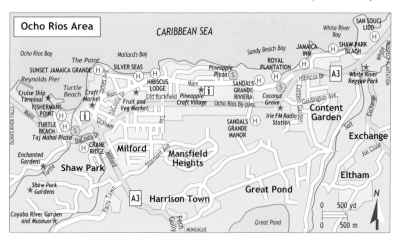

Ocho Rios Area

ment buildings, is built around the double curve of west-facing **Ocho Rios Bay**, sheltered by a northern promontory called **The Point**. East of the city centre is the Ocho Rios **Cruise Ship Dock**, which handles a steady flow of mainly US cruise vessels. Many of their passengers are drawn as if by magnetism straight from the pier into the purpose-built complex of pricey duty-free stores immediately across the A3 highway

from the cruise ship dock. A handful of resort hotels also occupy downtown sites overlooking the bay, but most of Ocho Rios's popular beach hotels are east of the city centre, spread out along the white sand beaches which stretch for kilometres along the north coast.

▲ *Above: The modern hotels of Ocho Rios are visible from Shaw Park Gardens.*

Turtle Beach and Mallard's Bay *

Turtle Beach, immediately north of the town centre, is a half-mile (1km) stretch of urban beach dominated by the four high-rise blocks of Turtle Beach Towers, a 122-apartment condominium complex. Not the best beach in Ochi. Separated from Turtle Beach and downtown Ochi by **The Point**, the beach at **Mallard's Bay** is cleaner and a little less built up, with white sand, water sports, and the large Hibiscus Lodge hotel at its eastern end.

Shaw Park *

Just off the A3, 1 mile (1.6km) from the town centre and located on the slopes south of downtown Ocho Rios lies **Shaw Park Gardens**. This magnificent expanse of landscaped garden covers 34 acres (14ha) of tropical trees, waterfalls and flowering shrubs, and is home to

OCHO RIOS COCKTAIL

Try this refreshing drink originating in Jamaica:
• One measure dark rum
• One measure guava juice or half cup diced guava
• Quarter measure lime juice
• 4 ice cubes
Blend all the ingredients until smooth. Serve chilled in a champagne glass.

▲ *Above: It's the experience of getting wet that counts at Dunn's River Falls.*

many colourful bird species. There are fine views of Ocho Rios Bay and the beaches. Open 08:00–17:00 (tel: 974 2723, www.shaw parkgardens.com).

Coyaba River Gardens and Mahoe Falls ★★★

Near Shaw Park, is a water garden and park with spectacular artificial and natural cascades over limestone rocks, a natural aquarium, fine sea views, a museum of island history and some outstanding examples of traditional architecture. Open 08:00–17:00 daily (tel: 974 6235, www.coyabagardens.com).

Dunn's River Falls ★★★

Two miles (3km) west of Ochi, is the region's longest established visitor attraction and has been given a new look with the addition of a range of modern facilities to enhance its gentle series of natural cataracts that cascade some 600ft (195m) to the sea. Falls guides lead a 'human chain' of visitors up the cataracts – the highest of which is less than 30ft (9m) high. Individual travellers should avoid 'cruising ship days' when the attraction is packed with hundreds of day visitors. Open normally 08:30–17:00, cruise ship days 07:00–17:00 (tel: 974 5944, www.dunnsriverfallsja.com).

Dolphin Cove at Treasure Reef ★

Next to Dunn's River Falls (and open same hours), Dolphin Cove may disturb those who feel it is wrong to pen dolphins so that humans may swim with them; the attraction also offers swimming with sharks and stingrays, and a boardwalk where fancy-dress pirates entertain visitors, who can also 'interact' with exotic birds and reptiles (www.dolphincovejamaica.com).

DEEP-SEA ANGLING

Jamaica is tops for deep-sea fishing, with big fish including **blue** and **white marlin**, **wahoo**, **tuna** and **dolphin** (dorado) waiting to take the bait only 15 minutes offshore, where Jamaica's reefs give way to blue ocean. Blue marlin can be caught year-round, though the best season is reckoned to be summer and autumn. The **Port Antonio Blue Marlin Tournament**, in October, is one of the Caribbean's top deep-sea angling events. Best places for boat charters are Montego Bay, Ocho Rios and Port Antonio.

Cranbrook Flower Forest *

Situated at Llandovery, St Ann's Bay, is a tranquil, so-called eco-tourism experience with tropical water gardens, a riverside walking trail and sections of rainforest; it also offers a range of activities including bird-watching, pond fishing, guided nature walks and volleyball. It is open daily 09:00–17:00 (tel: 995 3097, www.cranbrookff.com).

Green Grotto Caves *

Said to have provided refuge for escaped slaves in the 18th century, these limestone sea caves are a maze of passageways and caverns adorned by twisted rock formations. The tour includes a free drink. Open daily 09:00–16:00 (contact Discovery Bay, tel: 973 2841, www.greengrottocavesja.com).

Greencastle Estate Plantation Tour

In the foothills of the Blue Mountains, Greencastle is a working plantation that offers a hand-on experience of Jamaican rural life, as well as a tour of its stunning orchid houses and plantings. Open daily 09:30–17:00; Robins Bay, St Mary (tel: 881 6279, web: www.gcjamaica.com).

Prospect Plantation Butterfly World and Horseback Rides **

Formerly a working plantation founded in the 18th century, Prospect now features a riverside horseback ride through tropical forest and a butterfly 'aviary' made colourful by dozens of local species. It also has a pretty picnic area. Prospect Plantation, Ocho Rios, tel: 994 1058. Open daily 09:00–17:00 (www.prospectplantationtours.com).

▼ Below: Harmony Hall features Jamaican-style fretwork archways.

Harmony Hall ✶✶✶

This 150-year-old great house, 4 miles (7km) east of central Ocho Rios, was originally a Methodist manse and the hub of a pimento pepper estate. Restored and embellished in 1981, it now houses one of Jamaica's best art galleries, displaying fine arts and crafts from all over the Caribbean, with special emphasis on primitive and naïve painters and sculptors. It also has a good restaurant. Open Tue–Sun 10:00–17:30; Tower Isle, St Mary (tel: 974 2870, www.harmonyhall.com).

PORT MARIA

Port Maria, 20 miles (32km) east of Ocho Rios, is yet another former banana boom town which has fallen on hard times since the advent of bigger refrigerated cargo vessels (which its small harbour cannot handle) and roads to truck fruit to other ports. Unlike Port Antonio, which recouped its fortunes by pioneering Jamaican tourism, Port Maria has yet to become a hit with visitors to the island, despite its attractive setting on eastward-facing **Port Maria Bay**, a turquoise expanse of ocean framed by steep hills covered with woodland and plantations. The town itself has a few buildings of minor interest, but the main attractions are on the hills above and behind the port, where another of Jamaica's best-known, most loved and talented expatriates made his home.

Among Port Maria's older buildings is **St Mary's Parish Church**. Built of limestone in 1861, it has an attractive churchyard planted with nodding palm trees. Also of note, though rather neglected, is the **St Mary Court House** which dates from 1820. Immediately opposite the courts is the **Tacky Monument**, erected in memory of the rebel slave leader Tacky, who led the Easter Rebellion of 1760 that began in St Mary parish.

Firefly ★★★

Firefly, the Jamaican home of composer, musician, actor and playwright Sir Noel Coward, is 1½ miles (2km) north of Port Maria. Visit for high tea or Martini cocktails on the lawn, which boasts a breathtaking view over Port Maria Bay. **Island Outpost**, which administers the house as a unique museum on behalf of its owner, the Jamaican National Heritage Trust, has restored Firefly to look just as it was on the day Coward died – Sunday, 28 February 1965. Finishing touches include virtually every last detail, such as an unfinished painting by Coward on the easel in his studio and his silk dressing gown hanging on the bathroom door. One almost expects the great man, elegant as ever, to step, cocktail shaker in hand, onto the lawn. He won't, though, because he's buried under it. A plain white marble slab marks the grave. Open 09:00–17:00 daily (www.islandoutpost.com).

Brimmer Hall ★★★

Five miles (8km) southwest of Port Maria, this wooden Great House is surrounded by 700 acres (280ha) of plantations where grapefruit, coconut, pimento, sugar cane and bananas are grown. Built in 1817, it is decorated with colonial antiques. Open daily; two-hour guided tours of house and plantation start at 11:30, 13:30 and 15:30.

NOEL COWARD

Noel Coward (1899–1973) first came to Jamaica in 1950, and bought a villa which he named **Firefly** in the hills above **Port Maria** where he lived for much of the rest of his life. Famed for his dry wit and equally dry Martinis, Coward was incredibly prolific and a multi-talented actor, playwright, composer, producer, author and painter. Many of his paintings decorate the walls at Firefly, and the stunning land- and seascape surrounding the house inspired one of Coward's best-loved songs, *A Room with a View*.

▼ *Below: Largely passed by, Port Maria has not yet succumbed to tourism.*

Too many visitors meet Jamaicans only as service providers – whether waiters, taxi drivers, water-sport instructors, street vendors or ganja peddlers. To find out what Jamaicans are like at home, join the 'Meet the People' programme instituted by the **Jamaica Tourist Board**. More than 1000 Jamaican families have signed up to welcome visitors into their lives for a day or more. The programme is free to visitors, and the JTB will match you with hosts who share your interests.

ST ANN'S BAY

The quiet capital of the eponymous parish is all the quieter now that it has been bypassed by the recently upgraded coast highway and, with a scattering of colonial buildings – including the 19th-century courthouse – it is a pleasant stop en route between Ocho Rios and Montego Bay. Statues of two towering figures from Jamaican history stand on the main street, in the centre of St Ann's: the bronze statue of **Columbus**, the first European to put Jamaica on the map, was cast in Genoa, Columbus's birthplace, and the **Marcus Garvey Monument** commemorates St Ann's most famous son. Born in 1887, Garvey is now considered a Jamaican national hero because of his lifelong campaign to give African-Caribbean and African-American people a sense of their African roots.

Seville Great House *

This plantation manor was built in 1745 from stone recycled from the first Spanish settlement on the island, Sevilla la Nueva (New Seville) which stood half a mile (1km) west of St Ann's Bay. Founded in 1509 and abandoned in 1533, the Spanish settlement provided a source of dressed stone for a number of later settlers. Seville Great House is now a museum, and in the grounds stands the estate's sugar mill, molasses boiling house and water wheel. Open 09:00–17:00 daily (tel: 972 2191, www.jnht.com).

▶ Right: Marcus Garvey wanted to give descendants of African slaves pride in their roots.

Chukka Cove *

World-class polo, riding and show-jumping events are the main attractions at Jamaica's top equestrian centre. Chukka Cove also offers scenic horseback trails and riding packages, varying from two hours to three days of riding. Open 09:00–17:30 daily.

RUNAWAY BAY

Runaway Bay's name comes – according to some sources – from the flight of the escaping Spanish garrison following their defeat by the British in 1658. According to others, the place was favoured by runaway slaves because from here, in a stolen pirogue, it was only 90 miles (130km) to Cuba, where they might find refuge. Runaway Bay was little more than a name on the map until the development of tourism, but the fine beaches between the village itself and Salem, some 3 miles (5km) east, were bound to attract resort development, and a string of resort hotels now dominates this sector of the coast.

Cardiff Hall *

The Cardiff Hall Great House was built in 1789 by architecht, John Forsythe. The Great House, 1 mile (1.6km) east of Runaway Bay, was one of the first on the island, with one of Jamaica's largest sugar estates spread around it. A tour of the mansion gives some idea of the grandeur in which the 18th-century white Jamaican planters lived. The estate has now been developed, and includes the **Runaway Bay Golf Course**. Open 09:00–17:00 daily (www.runawaybay.com).

Runaway Caves **

West of Runaway Bay, en route to Discovery Bay, are limestone caverns which plunge as deep as 120ft (35m) underground. Guided tours on foot and by boat explore the partially flooded caves and their twisted stone formations. The tours include a boat trip across the underground lake known as **Green Grotto**. Tours 09:00–16:00 daily (tel: 973 2841, www.greengrottocavesja.com).

FRIENDS OF THE SEA

Non-profit organisation **Friends of the Sea**, which is dedicated to saving Jamaica's marine environment, has a list of rules for visitors to the island's seas, reefs and beaches:
• Don't touch or spear any marine life.
• Don't let your hands, feet, fins, scuba tank or boat anchor come into contact with any part of the delicate coral reef. Don't stand on coral heads.
• Don't take, or buy, starfish, conch shells, sea fans, coral or turtle products.
• Don't litter. Your trash is harmful to marine life as well as unsightly.
• Observe the closed season for lobsters – it is illegal for any restaurant to serve fresh lobster between 1 April and 30 June.

Bob Marley Mausoleum ***

Probably the best known Jamaican in history, Bob Marley was born at Nine Mile, 15 miles (24km) south of Runaway Bay, and was buried here following his death from a brain tumour in 1981. His mausoleum is on Mount Zion, on the site of the family home, a small wooden shack which has been rebuilt in stone in his memory. Marley's tomb, a slab of white Italian marble, is in a small chapel combining Ethiopian influences (like all Rastafarians, Marley believed in Ethiopia as his ancestral home) with pictures of Marley and his fellow Wailers, Rastafarian symbols, banners and badges. Outside is the 'inspiration stone' where Marley sat as a boy, before his family moved to Kingston when he was 13. It, and virtually everything else in the mausoleum compound, have been painted in the three symbolic colours of Rastafari – red, yellow and green. In the church, a leather funeral album contains the names of the thousands of people who joined Marley's funeral procession. Almost as many hustlers, higglers and 'guides' seem to lurk in the environs of the mausoleum. Open 09:00–17:00 daily (www.bobmarleymovement.com).

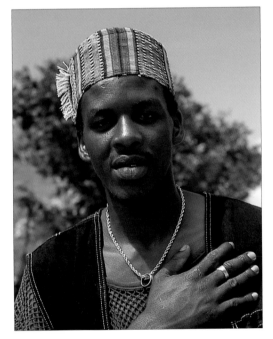

▼ *Below: A guide at the Bob Marley Mausoleum enthusiastically traces his hero's footsteps.*

DISCOVERY BAY

The location of Discovery Bay – straddling the main coast highway, with a gigantic bauxite shipping operation dominating its stretch of waterfront and narrow beach – has not helped it to develop as a tourism destination. There is little to see, but there are small guesthouses.

Columbus Park ★★

This open-air museum is perched above the shore, 1 mile (1.6km) west of Discovery Bay, on the spot where Columbus is said to have made his landfall in 1494. The museum's collection is eclectic and haphazard but nevertheless fascinating, with colonial cannon, bits and pieces from the old sugar refineries – including a water wheel – and other relics of the bygone and unlamented plantation era. Open 24 hours daily.

▲ *Above: Relics of Jamaica's past lie on display at Columbus Park.*
▼ *Below: Columbus is said to have made landfall at the site of Columbus Park in 1494.*

Puerto Seco Beach ★★

Across the road from Columbus Park, Puerto Seco is a well maintained public beach and a place to cool off if you are on an independent sightseeing outing along the north coast. The entry fee onto the gently shelving sand, offering safe, easy swimming, makes it worthwhile. Open 08:00–17:00 daily.

Best Times to Visit

Like the rest of Jamaica, this region's constant moderate climate allows visits virtually any time of the year.

Getting There

The north coast highway (A1/A3) connects **Ocho Rios** with **Montego Bay** (133 miles/180km) and **Port Antonio** (66 miles/100km). **Kingston** is 54 miles (89km) south on the A1. In 2011, Boscobel Aerodrome, outside Ocho Rios, reopened after a major redevelopment as **Ian Fleming International Airport**. When this edition was updated no flights were in operation from the UK, mainland Europe or North America, but Jamaica Air Shuttle (www.jamaicaairshuttle.com) is expected to begin service from Kingston (Tinson Pen) and Montego Bay really soon now.

Getting Around

Minibus services are crowded, irregular and unsafe, but **car hire** and **taxis** are available at all resorts. All-inclusive resorts also operate airport transfers to Montego Bay and **shuttle buses** into Ocho Rios.

Where to Stay

Ocho Rios

Luxury

Jamaica Inn Hotel, Main Street (Old Road), PO Box 1, Ocho Rios, tel: 974 2514, www.jamaicainn.com

Small, luxury, 45 rooms, own beach at Sandy Beach Bay; restaurant and bars.

Sandals Grande Riviera, Main Street, Ocho Rios, tel. 974 5691, www.sandals.com All-inclusive resort with choice of beachfront rooms and suites on half a mile of white sand beach or private villas in the hills above, sharing outstanding facilities including golf course, spa and water sports.

Shaw Park Beach Hotel, PO Box 17, Cutlass Bay, Ocho Rios, tel: 974 2552, www.shawparkbeachhotel.com Legendary luxury, 127 air-conditioned rooms overlooking White River Bay, tennis, water sports, pool, restaurant and three bars.

Mid-range

Hibiscus Lodge Hotel, 83 Main Street, Ocho Rios, tel: 974 2676, www.hibiscusjamaica.com Pretty, 26-room hotel on a rooftop location, five minutes' walk from Ocho Rios centre and the beach.

Budget

Crystal Ripple Beach Lodge, White River Bay, tel: 974 6132, www.crystalripple.com Small family hotel on a long white sand beach. Very good value for money.

Runaway Bay

Luxury

Royal Decameron Club Caribbean, Main Road, Runaway Bay, St Ann, tel: 973 4803, www.decameron.com Good value up-market all-inclusive resort with 135 beachfront cottages, excellent array of water sports, scuba-diving centre, tennis and gym, and three restaurants.

Breezes Runaway Bay , PO Box 58, Runaway Bay, St Ann, tel: 973 2436, www.breezes.com Successful family-oriented all-inclusive.

Mid-range

Bahia Principe, Salt Coopers, Runaway Bay, tel: 973 7000, www.bahia-principe.com Huge (834-room) all-suite resort with luxury facilities but some excellent bargain rates especially in low season.

Club Ambiance, PO Box 20 Runaway Bay, St Ann, tel: 973 6167, www.clubambiance.com Ocean views, health club, disco, restaurants and bars.

Franklyn D Resort, PO Box 201, Runaway Bay, St Ann, tel: 973 6987, www.fdrholidays.com Family-oriented all-inclusive, 67 suites; under 16s stay free.

Budget

Caribbean Isle Hotel, PO Box 119, Runaway Bay, tel: 973 2364, fax: 974 1706. 23 air-conditioned rooms, ocean views, pool, bar and restaurant, good service.

Pipers Cove Resort, Salem, Runaway Bay, tel: 973 7165, www.piperscoveresort

jamaica.com Small resort with 14 one-bedroom apartments, six studios, pool, restaurant, bar and private beach.

Orcabessa and Port Maria
LUXURY

Goldeneye, Oracabessa Beach, Oracabessa, tel: 946 1958 www.goldeneye.com Ian Fleming's Jamaican hide-away is now part of the Island Outposts empire and the hub of a villa resort development; sleeps eight guests, staff available by prior arrangement.

MID-RANGE

Casa Maria Hotel, Castle Gardens, Port Maria, tel: 725 0156, fax: 725 0157. Private beach, restaurants and bars.

WHERE TO EAT

Most visitors to the area stay in all-inclusive resorts or self-catering apartments. Away from Ocho Rios there are very few restaurants outside hotels, though there are plenty of fast-food outlets and jerk shacks. For places to eat away from Ochi, *see* Where to Stay.

Ocho Rios
LUXURY

Almond Tree, Hibiscus Lodge Hotel, 83–87 Main Street, tel: 974 2813. A la carte seafood, piano bar, live entertainment. **Evita's**, Ocho Rios, tel: 974 2333. A 19th-century mansion with Venetian cuisine, fresh

pasta and delicious desserts served indoors and outdoors. **Seafood Glant**, Main Street, Runaway, tel: 973 4801. Superb seafood and Jamaican cooking in the heart of Runaway Bay. **The Ruins at the Falls**, 17 Da Costa Drive, Main Street, Ocho Rios, tel: 974 8888. All-you-can-eat (and drink!) buffet lunch, a la carte dinner – and probably the best Jamaican and international dining in Ochi.

MID-RANGE

Glenn's Restaurant, Tower Cloisters, Ocho Rios, tel: 975 4360. Good value Jamaican specialities and international dishes such as pasta or burgers. **The Little Pub**, 59 Main Street, Ocho Rios, tel: 974 2324. Dinner theatre with cabaret in central Georgian-style complex. **Toscanini's**, Excellent Italian restaurant in the gracious surroundings of a former great house. Harmony Hall, Tower Isle, St Mary, tel: 975 4785.

BUDGET

Ocho Rios Jerk Centre, Da Costa Drive, Ocho Rios, tel: 974 2549. The best Jamaican jerk pork, chicken and seafood in town. Beware – it's very spicy.

TOURS AND EXCURSIONS

Blue Mountain Bicycle Tours, 121 Main Street, Ocho Rios,

tel: 974 7075, www.bmtours ja.com Downhill all the way through some of the most striking scenery in Jamaica, with a visit to the famous coffee plantations and a dip in a cascading waterfall. Tour includes transfers, brunch, lunch, bikes and guide. **Chukka Caribbean Adventures**, Ocho Rios, tel: 972 2506, www.chukka caribbean.com Mountain bike trips, four-wheel-drive safaris, river kayaking and tubing, and lots more soft adventure experiences. **Captain John's Island Hoppers**, Ocho Rios and the Blue Mountains from the air with Island Hoppers helicopter tours, tel: 974 1285, www.jamaica helicopterservices.com **Red Stripe Cruises**, Ocho Rios, tel: 974 4593. Sunbathing, snorkelling and sunset cruises and excursions to Dunn's River Falls. **Cool Runnings Catamarans**, Ocho Rios Pier, tel: 1954 376 7165, www.coolrunnings catamarans.com Party cruises and sunset trips aboard the sailing catamaran *Cool Runnings*.

USEFUL CONTACTS

Jamaica Tourist Board, Ocean Village Shopping Centre, tel: 974 2582/3. Advice and information on sightseeing, shopping, accommodation, restaurants, tours and beaches.

5
St James, Trelawny and Hanover

These three counties – Hanover in the west, St James in the centre and Trelawny in the east – make up the northern half of **Cornwall**. More than any other part, this region encapsulates the extremes of Jamaican life, from its biggest resort city, **Montego Bay**, to the forest strongholds of the **Cockpit Country**, where you can still almost hear the echoes of the far from welcoming Maroon slogan: 'Me no sen', you no come'. Montego Bay (called 'Mo Bay' for short) is thronged year-round by holiday-makers from North and South America and Europe and is one of the most popular ports of call in the Caribbean. The hills inland are punctuated with hotels, villas and resorts to suit all tastes, from some of the Caribbean's most expensive properties to value-for-money all-inclusives.

Mo Bay's international airport is the preferred gateway for most holiday-makers. Most of the area's largest hotels, many of them all-inclusive, are to be found on the fine beaches of the St James coast, west of Mo Bay, while the Trelawny coast is less intensively developed. East of Mo Bay, along the Hanover coast, are a string of up-market hideaways where you rub shoulders with the rich and famous. All around the region there are historic and purpose-built attractions to tempt you from the beach. Inland, **Hanover** and **St James** are covered by plantations and lush rolling hills, and the countryside is dotted with small farming villages. **Trelawny** parish is very different. South of the coastal plain, it rises steeply to form the rugged limestone mountains of the Cockpit Country, covered with thick jungle and still traversed by few roads.

CARIBBEAN SEA

DON'T MISS

*** **Montego Bay:** beaches, shopping, and lots of nightlife, wining and dining.
*** **Montego Bay Marine Park:** scuba, snorkelling and glass-bottom boat cruises.
*** **Bellefield Great House and Gardens:** authentically re-stored plantation Great House, just outside Montego Bay.
*** **Tryall Golf Club:** one of Jamaica's top resorts, with the Caribbean's finest golf course.
** **The Great River:** the island's longest river, venue for folklore and feasting.

◄ *Opposite: Rafting on the Martha Brae River.*

MONTEGO BAY

At first sight, Jamaica's second city seems to be reserved exclusively for the business of tourism, with souvenir markets, duty-free shopping, art galleries, and a host of bars and restaurants to cater to every taste – though the prices put them out of bounds to all but a handful of Jamaicans. The first Spanish settlers, who butchered semi-wild pigs and rendered their fat into lard, called their settlement Villa Manteca (literally 'Fat City'). Since corrupted into 'Montego' Bay, the name seems appropriate for a resort that boasts Jamaica's most finely tuned tourism money-making machine.

The city faces westward, overlooking the Bay, with the **Montego River** separating the city centre from the port and industrial area to the south. Montego Bay's beaches start within a mile of the city centre, and there are more than two dozen holiday hotels between central Mo Bay and Sir Donald Sangster International Airport, 2 miles (3km) north of the centre. Stretching off east along the St James coast are some of Jamaica's **best beaches** and certainly its biggest concentration of accommodation – some 40 per cent of the country's hotel rooms are in and around Montego Bay.

Montego Bay reaches a peak of excitement each August, when it hosts the annual **Reggae**

Sunsplash music fest, and year round it has probably the biggest choice of nightlife on the whole island. Visit town on 'Monday Night Out', when Gloucester Avenue is closed to traffic and becomes a multi-flavoured celebration of spicy Jamaican food and hot Jamaican music.

Sam Sharpe Square *

Montego Bay's city plaza is named after the leader of the slave rebellion in 1831. Now a national hero, Sharpe was captured and hanged with 500 others at Montego Bay. A statue in the square depicts Sharpe and another of Jamaica's national heroes, rebel leader Paul Bogle. **The Ring**, where slaves were auctioned, and **The Cage**, where runaways and unruly sailors were locked up, are other reminders of the bad old days. Sam Sharpe Square is also the focus of a straggling street market where stallholders sell colourful souvenirs, snacks and leisurewear. But to find out what Montego Bay is really about – white sand beaches – follow Gloucester Avenue north from the city centre.

SUNSPLASH

Invented to help put Jamaica back on the tourism map after the doldrums of the 1970s and 1980s – and to help boost visitor numbers in the summer low season – the **Reggae Sunsplash** has taken on a life of its own as one of the greatest gigs on the world music calendar, and certainly for musicians from all over the Caribbean and as far afield as the UK, South Africa and Zimbabwe. For six days and nights, with the sweet whiff of prime ganja drifting in the air, this is the place to hear reggae's biggest names – and plenty of soon-to-be-famous contenders – giving their best, and to discover what reggae is really all about.

◄ *Left: A dynamic tribute to rebel heroes in Sam Sharpe Square.*

Montego Bay's Beaches ★★★

The first of the famed beaches is **Walter Fletcher Beach**, less than half a mile from the middle of town and more popular with local people than with tourists. It is a public beach, which means there is an admission charge and facilities including changing rooms and a snack bar. As the first in a relatively long string, however, the beach itself is just a hint of what is still to come as you head north.

The **Doctor's Cave Beach**, about 1 mile (1.8km) from the centre, is Jamaica's first bathing beach.

Aquasol Theme Park ★★★

This privately operated beach and water-sports centre on Montego Bay's best beach offers snorkelling, jet skis, glass-bottom boat rides, tennis courts, a choice of places to eat and drink and after-dark entertainment. Open daily 09:00–midnight. Walter Fletcher Beach, Gloucester Avenue, Montego Bay (tel: 979 9447, www.aquasoljamaica.com).

Montego Bay Marine Park ★★★

The Marine Park comprises 10 sq miles ($26km^2$) of sea-grass beds, coral reefs, and coastal mangrove swamp stretching from the mouth of the **Great River**, west of Montego Bay, to **Dead End Point** near the airport. Scuba and snorkelling trips and glass-bottom boat cruises are offered by a number of companies in Mo Bay (tel: 952 5619, www.mbmp.org).

Bellefield Great House and Gardens ★★

Built in 1735, this Jamaican manor was once the headquarters of a plantation which included almost all the land on which Mo Bay now stands. Its founder, **Colonel Nicholas Jarrett**, was one of the officers of the British force which conquered Jamaica in 1655, and his descendants, the Kerr-Jarrett family, still own and work the 3000-acre (1200ha) estate. The **Great House** has been restored with exact attention to period detail, down to the rare books in the library and the pipes in the antique smoking cabinet. The estate has its own bar and barbecue restaurant. Open 09:00–17:00 daily for tours, advance booking required (tel: 952 2382, www.bellefieldgreathouse.com).

NOT A DOLPHIN!

Some visitors to Jamaica and the Caymans are appalled to see 'dolphin' on the menu. Don't panic – it's not a Flipper fillet. The dolphin in question is a large tropical fish, also called the **dorado** or, in the USA, **mahi mahi**. With its powerful predator's body and iridescent silver colouring, it is a handsome fish and a formidable adversary for sea anglers. On the other hand, the mahi mahi has never been known to act cute, entertain children, balance balls on its nose or rescue shipwrecked mariners. And it tastes great!

Bob Marley Centre ★★

Open for frequent reggae shows and other concerts, this is the original home of the annual **Reggae Sunsplash**, the world's biggest celebration of Jamaica's own music. Held each year in August, the event lasts a full week and attracts tens of thousands of reggae fans from all over Jamaica and the world.

Montego Bay Freeport ★★

The man-made, hammer-shaped **Freeport Peninsula**, which forms the southern bulwark of the bay, is made from sand dredged from the seabed to create the Montego Bay Freeport, where modern container ships and gigantic cruise liners dock. Immediately opposite the gleaming **Cruise Ship Terminal**, the **Montego Freeport Shopping Centre**, with its rows of duty-free outlets, allows cruise ship passengers to be separated from their money without ever straying more than a few hundred metres from their vessel. There are sandy beaches on the seaward side of the Freeport peninsula, where the **Seawind Beach Resort** operates a private nude beach for those averse to tan lines.

ST JAMES PARISH
ROCKLAND'S FEEDING SANCTUARY ★★

This privately owned bird sanctuary lies 7 miles (12km) west of town at Anchovy. The late Lisa Salmon, the original owner, began feeding and caring for local bird life 30 years ago, and hundreds of songsters now turn up for daily feeding time. The birds are so used to people that many of them will feed from your hands and, as Rockland's is almost 1000ft (300m) above sea level, you will also be rewarded by magnificent views of Montego Bay. Open 14:00–17:00 daily.

THE WHITE WITCH

Rose Hall Great House, near **Montego Bay**, is said to be haunted by **Annie Palmer**, whose first husband, John Palmer, built Rose Hall in 1770. According to legend, Annie – who had learned *obeah* from one of her slaves – first poisoned John, then went on to stab her second husband and strangle her third before taking a succession of slave lovers, whom she also murdered one by one, until the slaves finally rebelled and murdered her in 1833. Though there was a real Annie Palmer, there's not a shred of evidence to support this colourful story.

▼ *Below: The Montego River separates Montego Bay centre from the port.*

Belvedere Estate ★★

This working plantation about 12 miles (17km) south of Montego Bay covers more than 1000 acres (405ha), most of them covered with citrus and spice plantations. With its brooks and cascading waterfalls, it's a pleasant – and cool – way to escape from the hustle of Montego Bay. Open 10:00–15:30 Monday–Saturday.

Rose Hall Great House ★

The most famous of Jamaica's great plantation manor houses (which like most of them is said to be haunted) lay in ruins from 1830 until it was restored as a tourist attraction. It has now been born again as the core of a 7000-acre (2833ha) 'resort community' featuring luxury villas and hotels, including the Ritz-Carlton Golf & Spa Resort, and new 18-hole golf course, the Rose Hall Resort and Country Club and the Palmyra Resort and Spa, as well as 'The Shoppes at Rose Hall', a duty-free mall comprising 35 luxury boutiques (for information on tours and opening times, tel: 579 7973, www.rosehall.com).

Greenwood Great House ★★★

Built by the wealthy Browning family (from which the poetess **Elizabeth Barrett Browning** came), Greenwood is about 4 miles (7km) east of Montego Bay and boasts the best collection of antiques and artworks of any of the island's surviving Great Houses. It also has a fine collection of beautiful musical instruments, including a

St James, Trelawny and Hanover

magnificent rosewood piano commissioned by Edward VII. The house was built in the late 18th century, and tours of the house and surrounding plantation are available, led by guides dressed in period costume. Open 09:00–18:00 daily (tel: 953 1077, www.greenwood greathouse.com).

FALMOUTH

The heyday of this little harbour town – on the A1 north coast highway, 14 miles (23km) east of Montego Bay – was during the sugar boom of the late 18th century, when it grew into a thriving port graced by fine public and private buildings in Georgian style. Many of these survive, and indeed Falmouth today has Jamaica's best-preserved collection of buildings from this era. **Market Street**, in the town centre, is dotted with them. The most distinguished architectural survivals include the **Methodist Manse**, built in 1799 by the wealthy Barrett family; the 18th-century **Post Office**, and the early 19th-century **Courthouse**, fronted by doric columns and a final double external staircase but somewhat marred by a clumsy restoration after a fire in the 1920s.

J Charles Swaby Falmouth Swamp Safari *

Just 2 miles (1km) west of Falmouth on the A1, the main attraction of this purpose-built village are the captive-bred Jamaican crocodiles, which start out as cute bug-eyed critters about 6 inches (15cm) long and eventually grow into 7ft (2m) monsters – if they don't end up as handbags, belts or shoes. Also on show are birds, snakes, and cuddlier creatures at the petting zoo. In addition, there is a snack bar and jerk centre; tel: 929 9200, open Mon–Fri 09:00–16:30.

Martha Brae River ***

The Martha Brae flows out of the **Cockpit Country** hills to meet the Caribbean east of Falmouth. Trips down the river on a 30ft (10m) bamboo raft take about 75 minutes, ending at **Rafter's Village**, where there is a restaurant, bar, pool and shops.

MANATEE

It's hard to credit the ungainly manatee as the supposed inspiration for the legendary **mermaid**. Only about 100 of these harmless aquatic herbivores are believed to survive in Jamaican waters – most of them around the less-developed, swampy shores of the southeast. Growing up to 10ft (3m) long, manatees are still occasionally hunted for meat and, while there are legends of manatees rescuing shipwrecked sailors, some Jamaicans also believe a manatee swimming past a boat or house can render men and women infertile.

▶ *Right: Crocodiles sunbathe at the Jamaica Safari Village.*

THE DOCTOR BIRD

Jamaica's national bird is also one of its smallest. You'll see the **streamertail hummingbird** (*Trochilus polytmus*), or 'Doctor Bird', zipping around flower gardens or sipping nectar from flowers and feeder stations. Only 4½ inches (11.5cm) long without its streamer-like, 10-inch (25cm) tailfeathers, the male Doctor Bird's body is iridescent green, its crown and tail black, and its beak red. The female is less brightly coloured, without the streaming tail. Like other hummingbirds, the streamer-tail can hover in midair, fly straight up, down, sideways, and even go into reverse. Its in-flight hum is generated by wings which beat at almost 80 times every second when hovering – and up to 200 times per second in court-ship display.

Good Hope Estate ★★

This one-acre coconut and cattle plantation, 4 miles (7km) south of Falmouth, has marked trails for riding. **Good Hope Great House** was built in 1755 and, like so many of the sugar planters' mansions, fell into disuse in the early 20th century as the value of sugar dropped and the old plantation lifestyle ceased to be feasible. Good Hope was once the largest plantation on the island, covering 10,000 acres (4050ha). The estate has now been reduced to about 200 acres (80ha), but the Great House has taken on a new lease of life as a luxury hotel. With its fine Palladian architecture and Adam interior, the house must be one of the most attractive places to stay in Jamaica. Open 09:00–16:00 daily (tel: 469 3444, www.goodhopejamaica.com).

THE COCKPIT COUNTRY

Most of southern Trelawny parish is almost trackless wilderness. South of route B10 lies an area of almost 100 sq miles (260km²) of virtually trackless hill country, rising at its highest point, Cockpit Peak, to 2453ft (800m).

The Land of Look Behind ★

This is the home of the **Maroons**, the proud descendants of slaves of the Spanish who took to the woods and hills from the earliest days of European settlement and proved stubbornly hard for the British colonial forces to subdue. Looking at the Cockpit Country today, it's not hard to see why. The soft, porous limestone of this part of the island has sunk into a series of crater-like hollows, the so-called 'cockpits', interspersed with steep river gorges and choked with tropical vegetation. From their hill villages, the Maroons defied all who came against them. Their slogan came to be 'Me no sen', you no come', and in the 18th and early 19th centuries only the foolish went into this territory without a promise of safe conduct from the Maroon chiefs. Not for nothing is it still called the Land of Look Behind. The main Maroon settlement is at Accompong (*see* panel, p. 98).

Windsor Cave ★★

Unlike other, more easily reached caverns on the Jamaica coast, the Windsor Cave complex has not yet been seriously commercialised. Visitors must be accompanied by a Jamaica Conservation Development Trust warden (contact Windsor Research Centre to arrange a visit, tel: 997 3832, www.cockpitcountry.com). The small entrance leads into a two-mile (3km) labyrinth of limestone formations – take your own reliable flashlight, and be warned that this is no place for people with a fear of bats! The cave complex has not yet been fully charted, but is believed to be the source of the **Martha Brae River**, which reaches the sea near Falmouth. Open daily, no set hours.

HANOVER PARISH

West of Montego Bay, the coast of Hanover parish lacks the long beaches of the Mo Bay area, but is dotted with elegant resorts on private coves or on landscaped hillsides. Between **Sandy Bay** and **Lucea**, the biggest town in the parish, the Hanover coast is dominated by jagged cliffs, making Lucea's natural harbour a welcome sight for local fishermen.

> **ANANSI STORIES**
>
> One of the most enduring of Jamaica's original African traditions is the myth of **Anansi**, the cunning spider who usually gets the better of his adversaries – while never quite winning conclusively. The Anansi tales, and Anansi himself, originate in Ghana (formerly the **Gold Coast**, whence many slaves were brought). The dialect they are told in is peppered with words from several West African languages – and the same stories are told too in Ghana today. Among American slaves, Bra' (Brother) Anansi became Br'er Rabbit, and 'Please don't throw me into the briar patch' is a typical Anansi stratagem.

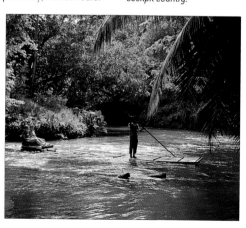

▼ *Below: The Martha Brae River runs down from the wild Cockpit Country.*

The Great River **

Flowing out of the limestone mountains of the hinterland, the Great River forms the parish boundary between **Hanover** and **St James**. To visitors accustomed to rivers on a European or North American scale, the name may seem inappropriate – the Great River is little over 50ft (15m) at its widest, but it is nevertheless the largest watercourse in the country. Lively night-time events – rum cocktails, dinner and a Jamaican folklore show – are held at the **Great River Feast Centre** close to the coast and, during the day, you can float downriver on a bamboo raft.

Tryall Golf Club ***

Jamaica's finest golf course, 12 miles (19km) west of Montego Bay, is on the site of a 19th-century sugar plantation, but immaculately groomed greens have taken the place of waving sugar cane. Tryall is respected by top golf professionals, who gather here each year to compete for golf's richest prize, the US$ 2.7 million World Championship. Tryall also offers some of Jamaica's most expensive and exclusive accommodation and a welcome mile-long (1.5km) beach (www.tryallclub.com).

▼ *Below: Tryall's water wheel, built 200 years ago to power plantation machinery, still turns today though it is no longer operational.*

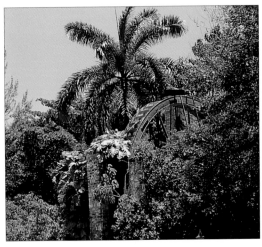

Tryall Water Wheel *

Tryall's most impressive historic landmark is the huge wood and cast-iron water wheel, a relic of the heyday of sugar when water was the major power source for plantation machinery. Built 200 years ago to harness the flow of the **Flint River**, the wheel still continues to turn, although it no longer powers anything.

◄ Left: Buildings of interest in the quiet town of Lucea include the courthouse, with its wooden clock tower and rounded cupola.

LUCEA

Hanover's capital of Lucea is a little town of wooden buildings with shaky-looking balconies and covered arcades. About 25 miles (40km) west of Mo Bay, the original sugar port is now the hub of farm land growing bananas, pimento, ginger, yams and sugar. There is little tourism here – most visitors usually only pass through on their way from Montego Bay to Negril – but there are some historic buildings of interest.

Fort Charlotte *

Lucea's original reason for existing was its location on the only decent anchorage on this stretch of coast, and this pocket-sized fortress was built to command and defend it. Overlooking Lucea harbour, the eight-sided fort mounted 20 cannon but never had occasion to fire them except on ceremonial occasions. Open daylight hours only.

Anglican Church *

The 18th-century church is one of Jamaica's oldest and contains a neo-classical monument to **Simon Clarke**, one of the wealthiest planters of the time, by the sculptor John Flaxman. Open daily.

FLORA AND FAUNA

Jamaica has some 3000 plant species, of which at least 800 are unique to the island, including hundreds of **orchids** and almost 600 species of **fern**. Wildlife is less varied, and many Jamaican species – the **manatee**, **crocodile**, **iguana** and **yellow boa** – are listed as endangered, along with several **bird** species. There's plenty of bird life, from **jungle parrots** to the vicious-looking **man of war** or **frigate** bird with its huge wingspan and razor beak, and the **'John Crow'**, or turkey buzzard, which despite its loathsome appearance does a good job of clearing the garbage from village middens, roadsides and beaches. At night, look out for 'rat-bats' as Jamaicans call **bats**, of which there are 25 species.

Jamaica's climate is moderate year-round, but the heat and humidity May–November, along with seasonal rains, make it officially off-season.

GETTING THERE

By air: Flights from the UK, mainland Europe, the US and Canada land at Donald Sangster International Airport (Montego Bay). Some flights continue to Kingston. Air taxi services are also available to Boscobel (Ocho Rios), Negril and Port Antonio.

GETTING AROUND

Resorts out of town operate shuttle **minibuses** to Mo Bay. **Taxis** run a fixed-fare system – agree the fare before boarding. Most resorts offer free or subsidised airport **transfers**.

WHERE TO STAY

Mo Bay area boasts 40% of Jamaica's hotel beds, including all-inclusives and beach resorts (St James and Trelawny) and up-market hotels (Hanover).

Montego Bay
LUXURY
Hilton Rose Hall Resort and Spa, Rose Hall Road, tel: 953 2650, www1.hilton.com Luxury all-inclusive resort next to the historic Rose Hall Plantation with on-site championship golf course and water park.
Sandals Inn, PO Box 412, Kent Avenue, Montego Bay, tel: 952 4140, fax: 952 6913. Intimate

couples-only 52-room all-inclusive; emphasis on personalised service.
Sandals Montego Bay, Kent Avenue, tel: 952 5510, www.sandals.com 244-room all-inclusive, sports, restaurants, bars, disco.

MID-RANGE
Doctors Cave Beach Hotel, PO Box 94, Montego Bay, tel: 952 4355, www.doctors cave.com Near beach, tennis, golf, riding, and Mo Bay markets; bar, restaurants, Coconut Grove restaurant is recommended.
El Greco Resort, 11 Queens Drive, PO Box 1624, Montego Bay, tel: 940 6116, www.el grecojamaica.com Apartment hotel fully equipped kitchens, maid service, satellite TV, pool, tennis.
Montego Bay Club Resort, Gloucester Avenue, tel: 952 3090, fax: 952 4639. Hotel near Doctor's Cave Beach; studios, suites; bars, restaurant, tennis, supermarket, boutiques.

BUDGET
Toby's Resort, 1 Kent Avenue, Montego Bay, tel: 952 4370, fax: 952 6591, www.toby resorts.com Affordable hotel with pool. Convenient for airport, shops and nightlife.
Wexford Court Hotel, 39 Gloucester Avenue, Montego Bay, tel: 952 2854, www.thewexfordhotel.com Rooms or studio apartments, self-catering facilities, restaurant and two bars.
St James and Trelawny Coast

LUXURY
The Atrium at Ironshore, PO Box 604, Ironshore, Montego Bay, tel: 953 2605, fax: 952 5641. Serviced apartments in gardens; restaurant and bar.
Breezes Rio Bueno Resort & Spa, Rio Bueno PO, Trelawny, tel: 954 0000, www.super clubs.com A 180-room all-inclusive, tennis, golf course, biggest pool in the Caribbean.
Coyaba Beach Resort and Club, Mahoe Bay, Little River, St James, tel: 953 9150, www.coyabaresortjamaica. com Full-service, 50 luxury rooms, private beach, restaurants, bars.
Good Hope Great House, PO Box 50, Trelawny, tel/fax: 954 3289, www. goodhopejamaica.com Luxurious, 10 rooms, gardens, pool, tennis, stables.
Half Moon Golf, Tennis and Beach Club, PO Box 80, Rose Hall, Montego Bay, tel: 953 2211, www.halfmoon. rockresorts.com Excellent sport facilities.

MID-RANGE
Cariblue Beach Hotel, PO Box 610, Ironshore, tel: 953 2250, www. cariblueresort.com Good value, 20 air-conditioned rooms, water sports, restaurant and two bars.

Hanover Coast
LUXURY
Round Hill Hotel and Villas, Hopewell, PO Box 64, Montego Bay, tel: 956 4050, www.roundhilljamaica.com

Chic rooms or villas, private beach, restaurant.

Tryall Golf, Tennis and Beach Resort, tel: 956 5660, www.tryallclub.com Elegant complex, 47 rooms and 49 villas on hillside; golf course, private beach, restaurants and bars. Most visitors eat at their hotels, but some restaurants offer a free transfer service to tempt you from your hotel. There is little variety beyond Mo Bay.

WHERE TO EAT

LUXURY

Great House Terrace, Tryall Club, tel: 956 5660. Probably the grandest restaurant in the area. Evenings only, reservations essential, dress code.

Bellfield 1794 Restaurant, Barrett Estate, Granville Main Road, Montego Bay, tel: 952 2382. Housed in a stone-walled, thatched building which was originally an estate sugar mill. Serves authentic Jamaican dishes such as fish escoveitch and curry goat.

Sugar Mill Restaurant, Half Moon Golf Course, tel: 953 2314. The massive old wheel of a sugar estate water mill dominates the Half Moon Golf Club's restaurant, which serves Caribbean and Continental dishes in elegant surroundings. Lunch and dinner.

MID-RANGE

Greenhouse Restaurant, Gloucester Avenue (next to Doctors Cave Beach Hotel), tel: 952 7838. Pizza, burgers, Jamaican specials.

Jimmy Buffet's Margaritaville, Gloucester Avenue, Montego Bay, tel: 952 4777. The Mo Bay outpost of this funky US chain, with sports bar and grill, hot tub, and water slide; cocktails, cold beer and Caribbean-American meals and snacks.

Marguerites Seafood by the Sea, Gloucester Avenue, tel: 952 4777. On the water's edge in the heart of Mo Bay's 'Hip Strip'; great steaks, unusually good range of vegetarian options. Dinner only.

Native Restaurant, 7 Queens Drive, Montego Bay, tel: 979 2769. Jamaican nouvelle cuisine.

The Pelican, Gloucester Avenue, tel: 952 3171. Local dishes, seafood; free transfers.

BUDGET

Native Jerk and **Garden Bar**, 56 Market Street, tel: 979 5063. Hot, spicy jerk dishes.

Rum Jungle Café and Bar, Coral Cliff Hotel, 165 Gloucester Avenue, tel: 952 4130. Open 24 hours; serves burgers, snacks and sandwiches and has a full bar.

The Groovy Grouper, Doctors Cave Beach, Gloucester Avenue, tel: 952 8287. Open all day, the Groovy Grouper serves Jamaican food and great burgers, with a seafod buffet Friday evenings.

The Pork Pit, Gloucester Avenue, tel: 952 1046. Jerk chicken, pork and fish. Craft markets on **Harbour**

Street (next to Sam Sharpe Square) and on **Fort Street**.

SHOPPING

Very up-market shopping at **Half Moon Shopping Village** at the Half Moon Hotel. The largest shopping centre in Montego Bay is the **Holiday Village**, opposite the Holiday Inn hotel.

TOURS AND EXCURSIONS

Accompong Maroon Tour, 32 Church Street, Montego Bay, tel: 952 4546 Tours of Accompong Town and St Elizabeth with visits to a bush doctor, Jamaican lunch and Maroon singers and dancers.

Braco Stables, Duncans, Trelawny, tel: 954 0185, www.bracostables.com Rides on the beach and through the scenery of the Braco estate.

Calico Pirate Cruises, White Sands, Montego Bay, tel: 952 5860, www.calicojamaica.net Snorkelling cruises in the Marine Park, trips to Margaritaville, sunset and dinner cruises – and unlimited punch, beer and soft drinks.

USEFUL CONTACTS

Jamaica Tourist Board, Cornwall Beach, tel: 952 4425.

Jamaica Union of Travellers Association (JUTA), Claude Clarke Avenue, Norwood, PO Box 1155, Montego Bay, tel: 979 0778, www.jutatoursltd.com

6
Westmoreland and St Elizabeth

Cornwall county's two southern parishes are very different from their north coast neighbours. **Negril**, on the very western tip of the island, is a thriving, fun-loving holiday resort, which started life as a tiny river-mouth fishing hamlet, became a backpacker's mecca in the 1960s, and then a fully fledged tourism destination in the 1980s. But the small towns and villages spread out along the south coast are far less developed, with only a scattering of hotels and guest-houses at **Bluefields** on the **Westmoreland** coast and **Black River** and **Treasure Beach** in **St Elizabeth**. This slow pace of growth is due to the relative inaccessibility of the two parishes, with the impenetrable Cockpit Country separating St Elizabeth from Trelawny parish to the north, and a rather winding and pot-holed coastal road connecting Negril and the south coast with Montego Bay.

Sightseeing attractions in Westmoreland and in St Elizabeth are generally natural or cultural rather than purpose-built. Nevertheless, most people heading for this area seek a beach holiday. Westmoreland's southern coastline is rocky and inaccessible for much of its length, but the parish's short stretch of west coast, which includes Jamaica's westernmost point, is occupied by **Negril Beach**, a 7-mile (11km) stretch of irresistible white sand. St Elizabeth, east of Westmoreland, is bound in the north by the wilderness of the Cockpit Country, and the northern part of the parish is the home of Jamaica's biggest **Maroon** community.

CARIBBEAN SEA

DON'T MISS

*** Negril: laid-back resort with the best beach in Jamaica.
*** Black River: venture into the **Great Morass** to see crocodiles, egrets and wild wetlands.
*** YS Falls: waterfalls tumble through lush wood-land on a working cattle farm.
** Bamboo Avenue: century-old giant bamboos shade miles of highway.
** Appleton Estate: see how fine rum is made and sample the product.

◀ *Opposite: Negril's magnificent beach stretches for 7 miles (11km).*

91

Although most of the town of Negril lies within Westmoreland, the parish line dividing Hanover and Westmoreland passes through Negril, and Negril Airport, Bloody Bay, part of Negril Beach and many of Negril's resorts and restaurants are technically part of Hanover.

▲ Above: A gentle evening cruise by sail past Negril Beach; the western extremity of Jamaica is renowned for its stunning sunsets.

NEGRIL

Magnificent sunsets, non-stop fun, and a youthful holiday clientele are the hallmarks of Jamaica's most westerly resort. This once tiny fishing settlement takes a little longer to get to than most other resort areas, and until fairly recently it was inaccessible enough to deter most visitors and developers. The stretch of white sand that makes Negril so popular now was one of the last Jamaican strands to be developed for tourism and, as late as the mid-1970s, this was a refuge for a handful of those in the know seeking a more relaxed getaway than offered by the big and bustling north coast resorts. Laid-back reggae and a whiff of ganja are still a part of the Negril scene, but the small, family-run guesthouses which were the pioneers of Negril tourism are gradually being ousted by bigger hotels, and there are few empty stretches on the sands of **Long Bay**.

Negril village proper is no more than a couple of streets with banks, shops, a tourist office, travel agencies and a few bars and restaurants on the south bank of the **Negril River**, which provides a sheltered anchorage for fishing boats. A long strip of tourist establishments continues south through the **West End** district to **South Negril Point**, where a lighthouse warns shipping away from the cliffs. A clutch of hotels, restaurants and guesthouses perches atop the cliffs, with views west over the Caribbean, and gathering to watch the spectacular sunset is a nightly ritual.

Negril's – and, indeed, Jamaica's – best beach starts north of the Negril River and stretches the length of Long Bay to **Rutland Point**, which separates Long Bay from a separate, smaller beach at **Bloody Bay**, once a pirate refuge. Hotels and guesthouses run along this whole stretch. Inland, a vast expanse of swampland known as the **Great Morass** is fast being drained and developed as Negril's tourism boom gathers pace. Negril is the place to go for the ultimate barefoot beach holiday, with fantastic sands, lots of water sports above and below the surface, lively nightlife and a great choice of places to stay, eat, and drink.

Development

Arguably, the area is showing some growing pains. The demands of tourism are stretching Negril's infrastructure to – and sometimes beyond – its limits, and improvements to roads, water supply, sewerage and electricity supply can cause the occasional hiccup. That said, Negril's developers claim they are determined not to repeat the excesses of tourism development elsewhere, and the town's building code aims to keep buildings below the height of the tallest palm tree, while extensive environmental studies are required before new construction is permitted. Offshore, Negril has more to offer snorkellers and scuba divers than most Jamaican resorts, with a long and well-preserved reef not far offshore. Though fishing and pollution resulting from attempts to drain the Negril wetlands have damaged the reef environment, parts of the reef have now been declared marine parks and efforts are being made to safeguard the marine life.

CALICO JACK

Negril was a favourite pirate anchorage, and some say the pirates' nasty habits gave **Bloody Bay** its name (though it more likely came from the whalers who butchered their catch here). **John Rackman**, or 'Calico Jack' (he got his name from his fondness for calico underwear), made it his base until 1726, when he was captured by **Captain Jonathan Barnet** of the Royal Navy and sent to the gallows at Port Royal. Among his crew were two female buccaneers, **Anne Bonney** and **Mary Read**, who by all accounts were just as tough as some of their crewmates.

▼ Below: The coast around Negril's West End is rocky, with cliffs reaching down to the blue sea.

▲ Above: Prized for its superb powder-like sand, Negril Beach is kept clean.

Negril Beach ★★★

As the finest beach in Jamaica, Negril Beach deserves every one of its three stars here. While many of Jamaica's most attractive strands have been privatised by up-market hotels or turned into city-operated pay beaches, Negril's is still open to all. Its 7-mile (11km) expanse of white coral sand is lined by hotels, guesthouses, food shacks, cocktail bars and more sophisticated restaurants, and the horizon is dotted with the sails of fishing boats, windsurfers, catamarans and cruising yachts. Every water sport under the sun is on offer. Along the beach, peddlers sell everything the visitor could wish for – from fresh coconuts and pineapple chunks to sunscreen, ganja and extra-large cigarette papers – and there's a rock-steady soundtrack of dub, reggae and roots rock day and night.

You can eat and drink in a different spot at every meal for a fortnight and still have new places to visit, and – despite Negril's rapid growth into a full-fledged resort – the atmosphere is distinctly more laid-back than in any other Jamaican resort. Tourism has become a way of life. The beach is patrolled by plainclothes police officers on electric golf carts, and while a late night stroll is not advisable, you can stroll along the beach for miles during the day and evening without significant hassle.

At the south end of Negril Beach, just across the river from the village centre, the market vendors sell carved ornaments, beachwear, weaving, artwork and snacks. Open 08:00 to sunset daily.

ARTIFICIAL REEFS

After a seven-year campaign, funds were granted to create the **Negril Marine Park** in 1996. The **Negril Coral Reef Preservation Society** already has 36 permanent reef mooring buoys in **Long Bay** so that boats no longer anchor on the reef. Jamaica is also in the forefront of a high-tech coral reef regeneration project. Marine biologists have discovered that corals can be persuaded to take root and grow faster on a metal framework if a trickle of electric current is passed through it to speed up mineral deposits from surrounding sea water.

Booby Cay **

At the north end of Negril Beach, **Rutland Point** juts out into the Caribbean, separating **Long Bay** from smaller **Bloody Bay**, a palm-fringed crescent of sand which once provided an anchorage and careenage for buccaneers such as the renowned Calico Jack Rackham – and for whalers, who butchered their catch here, giving the bay its rather gruesome name. Just offshore, the tiny island of Booby Cay is like the typical desert island depicted in cartoons – just a few boulders, a ring of sand, and a cluster of lonely palm trees. Used as a location for Disney's version of *20,000 Leagues under the Sea*, it is named for the gannet-like booby birds which once nested there. You can rent a canoe, sailboat or jet ski at Negril Beach to visit the island, which offers good snorkelling around its rocky shores, or take a half-day sailing cruise from Negril.

Negril Lighthouse *

Just to the south of the cliffs of **South Negril Point**, the lighthouse was built in 1836, when its lantern ran on paraffin. This is Negril's only historic site, although the view from the westernmost point of the island is more impressive than the lighthouse itself.

It is open by special arrangement only; contact the Jamaican Tourist Board in Negril.

WESTMORELAND PARISH

Westmoreland is a rural parish of farms and plantations. With few beaches and undramatic scenery, it has few lures for the visitor. **Savanna-la-Mar**, the parish capital, is an unexciting commercial centres, while **Bluefields** is a ramshackle fishing settlement with a good beach but few places to stay. The only sign of full-scale tourism development on this stretch of the coast is the new Sandals all-inclusive resort at **Whitehouse**, west of Bluefields.

Westmoreland is similarly bereft of big-league tourism attractions, but hardcore reggae fans make a pilgrimage to **Belmont**, the birthplace of reggae

> **VANISHING WETLANDS**
>
> Inland from Negril's seven miles of sandy beach lies a less well-known environmental asset – the 6000-acre (2430ha) wetland known as the Great Morass (there are in fact two wetland areas with this name: one at Negril, the second inland from Black River). Fed by the **Orange** and **Fish** rivers, the swamplands are a giant filter, absorbing the silt that washes down off the hills, and protecting Negril's coral reef from being stifled under gallons of mud.

▼ *Below: The lighthouse at Negril.*

ROYAL PALMS

Among Jamaica's most striking trees is the graceful royal palm, an emblem of the island for many visitors. The world's largest concentration of Jamaican royal palms is within the Great Morass outside Negril (not to be confused with the Great Morass by the Black River) where a 250-acre (100ha) expanse of wetlands has been set aside as a reserve. The reserve there was created in the early 1980s after an upsurge of popular protest against plans by the owner, the **Petroleum Corporation of Jamaica**, to use it for peat-mining. It is now managed as a protected conservation area by the **Negril Environmental Protection Trust**.

legend Peter 'Tosh' McIntosh (1944–87), where a small memorial garden is being developed by his family; it is open only irregularly.

ST ELIZABETH PARISH

West of Westmoreland, St Elizabeth is Jamaica's last tourism frontier, with an array of sights and activities striking landscapes and beaches that have so far escaped Negril-style development, and where fishing, farming and a traditional way of life still provide most local people with a living.

Inland lies the impenetrable **Cockpit Country**, homeland of the **Maroons** who resisted conquest from this mountain fastness for centuries (see p. 13). The drive to **Accompong**, their main settlement, is spectacular.

Black River and the Great Morass ★★★

Now a cheerfully ramshackle fishing port with a surprising array of traditional and colonial buildings, Black River grew wealthy on the logwood trade in the 19th century and was the first place in Jamaica to see electric lighting. The key to its prosperity is Jamaica's longest river, which flows 44 miles (72km) through the Great Morass, the largest wetland area in the Caribbean. The rivers owes its name to the black mud that covers its bed, making its water look black though

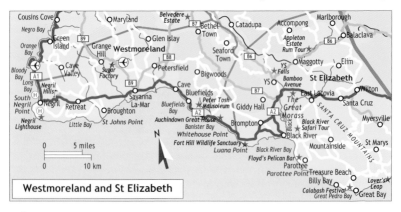

Westmoreland and St Elizabeth

in fact it is very clear – allowing an excellent view of the rare Jamaican crocodiles for which the morass is a last refuge. It also shelters more than 100 species of bird and a host of other wildlife. Local fishermen work the river from wooden dug-out canoes, sharing the water with the crocodiles – some of which grow up to 14ft (4m) long.

▲ *Above: Fishing boats lie moored at the mouth of the Black River.*

The Great Morass can be explored by boat from the Black River (*see* Tours and Excursions p. 101). The town also has two historic and charming hotels – the **Waterloo Guest House** (the first building in Jamaica to boast electric light) and **Invercauld Great House**, originally the 19th century home of a wealthy merchant. Both are interesting examples of Jamaican architecture and are worth looking at even for those who do not plan to stay overnight. Black River's most delightfully eccentric attraction, however, lies about a mile offshore. The **Pelican Bar** is a ramshackle affair built of mangrove poles, thatch and driftwood that stands on stilts in waist-deep water where stingrays swim and pelicans plummet. It look flimsy, but has survived at least two hurricanes.

YS Falls ★★★

This 2500-acre (1012ha) farm at Middle Quarters, 8 miles (12km) north of Black River, with thoroughbred racehorses, pedigree Red Poll cattle, and papaya plantations was founded by John Yates and Richard Scott in 1684 and takes its name from their initials. Run by the Browne family since 1887, its main attraction is a series of seven cascades that tumble through lush woodland scenery. Visitors can swim in 20 waterfall pools and stroll on paths lined with bamboo, red ginger

CROCODILES

The Jamaican crocodile (often, and incorrectly, called 'alligator') is one of the world's rarest. A glance at the map, with its scattering of placenames like **Alligator Pond** and **Alligator Hole**, is a hint that these leathery leviathans were once much more numerous. The biggest threats to the Jamaican croc today are theft of its eggs, which are sometimes eaten, and more importantly the rapid destruction of its wetland habitats. The best place to see crocodiles is on the **Black River**, which has the largest breeding population on the island and where some crocodiles have become so used to visitors that they can even be touched.

MAROON REBELS

Many Maroons were experienced warriors, sold into slavery by their African enemies after defeat in battle, and none had any reason to love their white masters. Their charismatic leader **Cudjoe** became the greatest of Maroon chiefs. Rather than attempt to confront enemy British troops and island militia in open country – where European firearms put them at a disadvantage – the Maroons chose to fight in the thick forests of the **Cockpit Country** and the **Blue Mountains**. Here their skill in ambush, led by Cudjoe, made them virtually invincible.

and scarlet-flowered bird of paradise shrubs. Open 09:30–15:30 Tuesday–Sunday (www.ysfalls.com).

Appleton Estate ★★★

Rum and Jamaica go together, and this distillery and sugar cane plantation at Siloah, in the lovely Black River Valley, attract visitors from all over the island to see sugar being turned into rum at the islands biggest distillery, the heart of the J. Wray and Nephew Ltd. operation since the mid-18th century. Rum is aged in thousands of oak barrels, and the plantation covers more than 4000 acres (1620ha).

Tours Monday–Saturday, including welcome rum punch, rum sampling and a bottle of rum to take away. For those who haven't had enough rum, there is also a rum shop and a rum bar.

Treasure Beach ★★★

Treasure Beach is simply the most delightful place to stay on the south coast, with a string of three sandy

▶ *Right: Greenery covers a series of cascades on the YS River in St Elizabeth parish; the river takes its name from the initials of the original owners of the surrounding land.*

beaches – **Billy Bay**, **Frenchman Bay** and **Calabash Bay** separated by rocky headlands and overlooked by a sprinkling of stylish small hotels, gorgeous villas and budget guesthouses. The village spreads along several miles of country road, with houses separated by fields and farms, and there seems to be a small rum shop, restaurant or bar at every turn in the road.

▲ *Above: From Lovers' Leap on the south coast there are extensive views along the shore and inland.*

Local people are among the friendliest in the island, and walking along the beach or in the countryside is pleasantly hassle-free in comparison with other resorts, while crime – though not unheard of – is certainly much rarer than elsewhere. Fleets of brightly coloured fishing boats land their catch each day, and you can buy fresh fish or lobster straight off the boat. There's none of the hardcore nightlife that draws ravers to Negril, but there are enough small local nightclub bars playing reggae every Friday and Saturday. Basic water sports – including sea kayaks – are available, and several local skippers operate trips by high-speed launch to **Black River**, the legendary **Pelican Bar** and into the wetlands of the **Great Morass**. Just inland of the village is a large, brackish-water lagoon that seasonally attracts large numbers of wading birds, and dolphins are often seen just offshore, while echelons of pelicans glide overhead at rooftop height.

Lovers' Leap *

Lovers' Leap with its red and white lighthouse 1500ft (460m) above the sea offers spectacular views of the coast and the Santa Cruz Mountains. Legend attributes the name to a suicide love pact between two slaves who threw themselves from the cliff rather than be separated.

DUPPIES

Given the island's bloody history, from the ruthless extermination of the Arawaks through to the slave uprisings, battles between Britons and Spaniards, the buccaneering era and the Maroon wars, it's hardly surprising that many Jamaicans retain a belief in 'duppies' – the spirits of those who have come to a violent end, doomed to walk the night forever. Among them are the ghosts of **Lovers' Leap**, on the St Elizabeth coast, where two slave sweethearts are said to have jumped to their deaths rather than be separated, while Bob Marley's track *Duppy Conqueror* is a celebration of the man who walks unafraid of his fate.

BEST TIMES TO VISIT

Jamaica's climate is moderate year-round, but the heat and humidity May–November, along with seasonal rains, make it officially off-season.

GETTING THERE

By **road**, Negril is 52 miles (81km) from Mo Bay on the A1 and 153 miles (240km) from Kingston on the A2. No public road transport, but JUTA (*see* Useful Contacts, p. 89) runs shuttle **buses** to Mo Bay. **Air Jamaica** flies to Negril from Montego Bay and Kingston.

GETTING AROUND

24hr taxis cruise hotels and nightspots in Negril, and there is a taxi rank at Adrija Plaza. Hire **bicycles** and **motorcycles** at hotels and outlets in Negril. Jeep and **car hire** is also available.

WHERE TO STAY

Negril
LUXURY
Rockhouse Hotel, West End, Negril, tel: 957 4373, web: www.rockhousehotel.com Award-winning collection of stone-built, thatched villas with great sunset views, lovely pool and an excellent restaurant.
Sandals Negril, Norman Manley Blvd, tel: 957 5216, www.sandals.com Couples-only, all-inclusive resort on its own section of beach.
Tensing Pen, West End, Negril, tel: 957 0387, fax: 957 0161, web: www.tensingpen.com Exemplary boutique hotel

with rooms in thatched stone cottages and excellent service.

MID-RANGE
Beach House Hotel and Villas, Seven Mile Beach, Negril, tel (international toll-free): 1801 363 3529, www.negril-hotels.com Self-catering studios, one-bedroom apartments and villas on the beach, with housekeeping, laundry, bar and restaurant and (on request) nanny and babysitting services.
Country Country, Norman Manley Blvd, tel: 957 4273, www.countryjamaica.com Cottages combining cosy simplicity with modern facilities such as air conditioning and satellite TV, a great beach restaurant and a perfect location. Highly recommended.
Rondel Village, Norman Manley Blvd, tel: 957 4413, fax: 957 4915, web: www.rondelvillage.com Very comfortable, highly recommended choice of rooms, one- to three-bedroom villa suites with pool, beach-front restaurant, high-speed Internet access. Midway along Seven Mile Beach.
Sea Splash, Norman Manley Blvd, tel: 254 2786, www.seasplash.com Intimate beach hotel with excellent restaurant.

BUDGET
Villa La Cage, West End, Negril, tel: 957 4114, www.villalacage.com At higher end of budget range, with pool, restaurant, and choice of fan rooms, air-conditioned or de luxe rooms.

Ansell's Thatch Walk Cottages, Negril Beach, tel: 957 3419, www.ansellsthatchwalk.com Cosy self-catering cottages, some air conditioned, near the Negril Village end of the beach.
Yellow Bird Rooms & Cottages, Negril Beach, tel: 957 4252, www.theyellowbird.com Friendly, comfortable, long-established guesthouse on Seven Mile Beach.
Westlea Cabins, Negril Beach, tel: 957 4422. Basic but friendly accommodation midway along Negril beach offers rooms, restaurant and bar at rock bottom prices.

Treasure Beach
LUXURY
Doubloon Villa, Calabash Bay, tel: 965 0126, web: www.treasurebeach.net Superb, recently refurbished and air conditioned villa with pool and gardens overlooking magnificent beach. Cook, housekeeper and caretaker, satellite TV and wireless Internet access. Unbelievably good value for up to six people.
Sparkling Waters Villas, Billy Bay, web: www.treasurebeach.net Choice of three villas overlooking the sea above Billy Bay, with cook/housekeeper and caretaker, air conditioning, beautiful gardens, shared pool and unbeatable views.
Jake's Village, Calabash Bay, tel: 985 0557, www.jakeshotel.com Unique, highly

rated collection of colourful luxury cottages right in the heart of Treasure Beach, with its own fine restaurant.

MID-RANGE

Mar Blue, Calabash Bay, tel/fax: 965 3408, web: www.treasurebeach.net Outstanding new boutique hotel with a choice of rooms and suites, two pools and award-winning restaurant. **Taino Cove Hotel**, Old Wharf, tel: 965 3893, www.tainocove.com Brand new hotel with a big pool and fine poolside bar, overlooking a long white sand beach; all rooms air conditioned and stylishly decorated.

BUDGET

Ital Rest, Great Bay, tel: 965 0126, web: www.treasure beach.net Strictly for lovers of ultimate simplicity, these thatched cabins set amid palms and lush gardens is the most peaceful place in Jamaica.

WHERE TO EAT

Negril

LUXURY

Kuyaba Beach Restaurant and Bar, Norman Manley Boulevard, tel 957 4318. Fine food throughout the day and in the evening in stunning exotic surroundings on the beach. Free pick up from your hotel. **Negril**, tel: 957 4041. European and classical cuisine combined with new Jamaican influences. Open-air dining.

La Vendome, Charela Inn, Norman Manley Blvd, tel: 957 4273, www.levendome.com Fine dining, French/Jamaican food, fine wine list, live music.

MID-RANGE

Country Country Bar & Grill, Norman Manley Boulevard, Negril, tel: 957 4273. Beach restaurant seving seafood, vegetarian, and Chinese dishes. **Rick's Café**, West End Road, Negril, tel: 957 0380. This legendary Negril hangout has recently been renovated and is still a great place to chill, watch the sunset and admire the famous cliff divers. **Alfred's Ocean Palace**, Norman Manley Blvd, Negril, tel: 957 4669. A local legend since the 1970s, Alfred's family-run seafood restaurant, bar and nightspot continues to attract a loyal clientele, as well as big-name performers. See www.alfreds.com for up-coming live acts.

Black River

Pelican Bar, one mile offshore from Black River waterfront, tel: 354 4218. Outstanding location and unbeatable views from this shack on stilts on a shallow reef; limited menu, but the fish and lobster are excellent. A must.

Treasure Beach

Jack Sprat, Frenchman's Bay, Treasure Beach, tel: 965 3583. Outdoor dining, great Jamaican seafood, good pizza; right on the beach, with kayaks to rent.

TOURS AND EXCURSIONS

Funtours Jamaica, tel: 383 0152, www.funtoursjamaica. com Trips to the Royal Palms Reserve, half-day inflatable boat sea safaris, beach parties, longer tours all over the island. **Captain Dennis**, contact via Treasure Tours, tel: 965 0126. Fishing trips, boat trips to Black River from Treasure Beach. **Charles Swaby's Black River Safari**, 1 Crane Rd, Black River, tel: 965 2513. Boat tours up the river and into the Great Morass. **Negril Scuba Centre**, Mariners Negril Beach Club, tel: 965 4425, www.negrilscuba.com Resort courses and range of dives for certified divers, free hotel transfers, based in Negril for more than 20 years. **Ocean Tours Water Sports**, Fisherman's Club, Negril Beach, tel: 957 4693. Reef tours, cave cruises, Booby Cay island picnics, sunset cruises, fishing and snorkelling trips, waterskiing, banana boat rides, jet ski rental and parascending.

USEFUL CONTACTS

Easy Going Cabs, West End Road, Negril, tel: 957 3227. Airport shuttle, local journeys, 24hr service. **Treasure Tours**, Calabash Bay, Treasure Beach, tel: 965 0126, web: www.treasure beach.net Based in Treasure Beach, the only JTB-approved tour operator on the South Coast offers the widest choice of accommodation, tailor-made tours and excursions and airport transfers.

7. Manchester, Clarendon and St Catherine

The parishes of Middlesex are the island's most populous, with three large farming and commercial towns, but the south coast west of Kingston sees fewer tourists than any other part of the Jamaica – because it has fewer outstanding beaches and few decent roads. The A2 route runs east and inland through **Manchester** and **Clarendon**, leaving the south shore intriguingly hard to get to. Though rich in history – **Spanish Town** was Jamaica's first sizeable settlement and its seat of government until Kingston became the capital – the three parishes are not over-endowed with natural or man-made attractions, and for most visitors to the island they are points to pass through en route between brighter, busier resorts.

Nevertheless, they are places where you can see a side of Jamaica very different from the resorts and sightseeing experiences offered by the commercialised north shore. In the villages and towns of the south people live a lifestyle largely immune from the impact of multimillion-dollar tourism and the fast-paced, fast-changing fashions of Kingston. This is largely farming country, with cattle ranches and citrus, spice and coffee plantations, while the fishing settlements dotted around the coast show little sign of being transformed into holiday resorts. If you have a rugged enough vehicle and are prepared to brave the poorly surfaced and mostly signpost-free roads leading to the south coast, you'll find the last stretches of undeveloped shoreline in Jamaica. Alternatively, if you venture into the hills above **Mandeville** you will be rewarded with cool breezes and outstanding views.

DON'T MISS

*** **Cathedral of St Jago de la Vega:** Jamaica's most beautiful church.
** **White Marl Arawak Museum:** recreation of Arawak life.
** **Hellshire Beaches:** the best and busiest resorts.
** **Williamsfield Great House:** restored plantation manor house.
** **High Mountain Coffee Factory:** see coffee being processed from the field.
* **Marshall's Pen Great House:** historic home on a working estate; great for birdwatching.

◄ *Opposite: The cloistered arcades of the old Records Office in Spanish Town.*

MANDEVILLE AND SURROUNDS

Mandeville ★★

High among the **Don Figuerero Mountains** (named after one of the Spanish conquistadors), Mandeville has a cooler climate than the coast, thanks to an elevation of almost 2100ft (630m). The average local temperatures are around 3C° (6F°) cooler than at sea level, with daytime temperatures no higher than 27°C (80°F). This has always made it a popular getaway spot for wealthier Kingstonians, who visit to play a round of golf at the **Manchester Club** or go riding in the surrounding hills, and has led to the description of the town as 'more English than England' – presumably by someone who never set foot outside Jamaica. There's nothing English about Mandeville – not even the climate, which is far more pleasant than anything the UK has to offer. North of town the scenery is a little marred by the largest open-cast bauxite mine in the world and an alumina processing mill.

Manchester, Clarendon and St Catherine

Only 57 miles (89km) from Kingston on the A1, Mandeville is even attracting middle-class Jamaicans away from the heat and stress of the city, and many new residential homes have been built on the outskirts of town. Coffee and spices grow well in the hill country around Mandeville, and among the town sights are two factories producing some of Jamaica's best-known export delicacies – fine coffee and piquant sauces and pickles.

▲ *Above: Mandeville's comparatively cool climate made it a popular refuge for affluent Kingstonians in previous centuries, who settled here in numbers and built opulent homes in the surrounding hill country.*

Williamsfield Great House ★★

North of the town centre, Williamsfield Great House is an immaculately restored example of the plantation manor, built in 1770 by **Captain George Heron**, one of the biggest landowners in Manchester parish, where he lorded it over a 10,000-acre (4047ha) estate. Inside, paintings, furniture and decorations reflect the grandeur of the 18th-century sugar planter's way of life. Tours by arrangement only.

High Mountain Coffee Factory ★★

Also at Williamsfield, visitors may watch coffee being processed – from treating the green berries through the roasting and grinding process to sealing and packaging. The tours, by appointment only, provide a fascinating insight into this everyday commodity (www.high mountaincoffee10k.com).

Pickapeppa Factory ★★

Just a little further north of Williamsfield, at **Shooter's Hill**, the Pickapeppa Factory will appeal to anyone with a taste for spicy sauces. Pickapeppa makes a range of delicious pickles, flavourings and sauces from the many different tropical spices growing in Jamaica, but the exact recipe is kept top secret. Tours of the factory and plantations are by arrangement only (www. pickapeppajamaica.com).

Marshall's Pen Great House **

Around 2½ miles (4km) northwest of the town centre, at **Hibiscus Gardens**, Marshall's Pen Great House is still the headquarters of a working cattle estate. Its extensive woods and fields are a refuge for many Jamaican bird species, some of them rare, and owner Robert Sutton is a renowned expert on Jamaican birds. Tours of the house and grounds are by prior arrangement only.

Christiana *

This small town 13 miles (21km) north of Mandeville is 2900ft (950m) above sea level and set among cool, green surroundings. The scenery is well worth the 20-minute drive and, if you are touring the island by car, Christiana is an ideal place to spend a night. With its panoramic views, Christiana boasts one of the most pleasant small hotels in Jamaica.

▶ Right: One of the plantation houses around Mandeville, Marshall's Pen Great House, is still the centre of a working cattle estate; splendid wooden beams line the interior of the house.

SOUTH COAST
Long Bay
Head west from **Milk River**, past the rather scruffy fishing settlement of **Farquhar's Beach** and you will come upon the last long stretch of undeveloped beach in Jamaica – a 15-mile (24km) sweep of coastline which looks much as it must have done before the Spaniards arrived. An unsurfaced and deeply pot-holed track follows the coastline along Long Bay to picturesque **Old Woman's Point** and on to **Alligator Pond**, a fishing village which has the only accommodation on this stretch of coast.

Milk River Bath *
On the south coast of **Clarendon** parish, 18 miles (28km) south of **May Pen**, Milk River Bath's claim to fame is its radioactive thermal spring, claimed to alleviate aches, pains and skin infections. The spring's healing properties are said to have been discovered by a slave who had been beaten almost to death (a similar story is told about the spa at Bath, in St Thomas parish, see p. 56) and whose wounds were healed by immersion in the hot waters. The public baths and thermal swimming pool of **Milk River Spa** are open 10:00–18:00 weekends and public holidays.

MAY PEN
May Pen is a small commercial and farming town in the heart of Clarendon parish, 20 miles (32km) west of Spanish Town and set among some of Jamaica's richest agricultural land. The Denbigh Agricultural and Industrial Show, the biggest event of the year for Jamaica's farmers, is held at May Pen every August.

Halse Hall *
Built in the 17th century by **Thomas Halse**, who was one of the earliest British settlers, Halse Hall is a gracious building in limestone with wooden balconies and verandas. Recent restoration has returned much of its former grandeur, and it is beautifully furnished with colonial antiques. It is open to visitors by prior arrangement only.

RASTAFARI

Born in the 1930s, Rastafarianism is a melange of Old Testament Christianity, back-to-Africa fundamentalism and ganja-fuelled mysticism. It identifies African-Caribbean people with the enslaved **Israelites**, and white culture with **Babylon**. **Haile Selassie**, Emperor of Ethiopia (one of whose titles was **Ras Tafari**, meaning 'lion prince'), was venerated by Rastas as a living god. Ruler of the only African nation free of white rulers, he was a potent symbol of black pride. Real Rastas try to live in self-sufficient communities independent of 'Babylon' (one such group still struggles along in Ethiopia, 30 years after its foundation on land granted by Haile Selassie), but there are plenty whose commitment goes no deeper than growing the mandatory matted 'dreadlocks' and smoking ganja, regarded by true Rastas as a sacrament.

CHRISTOPHER COLUMBUS

Why do we still call the Caribbean the **West Indies** and its people **West Indians**? It's all due to Christopher Columbus. Born around 1450, Columbus went to sea aged 14, and became captain of his own ships trading between the Mediterranean and the Atlantic islands. Convinced that sailing westward would bring him to **Asia**, he persuaded **King Ferdinand** and **Queen Isabella** of **Spain** to finance his voyages of exploration. His second expedition, in 1493, brought him to Jamaica. Over the next decade he explored the Caribbean, while insisting that this was in fact Asia – 'the Indies'. In 1503, his ships returned to Jamaica after an arduous voyage from Darien (Panama) and spent almost a year making repairs. He eventually returned to Spain, where he died in May 1506.

Colbeck Castle *

Just outside the village of **Old Harbour**, 13 miles (20km) west of Spanish Town, and once one of the most imposing of Jamaica's mansion houses, Colbeck Castle is now a ruin standing among sugar cane and tobacco fields. Its builder, **Colonel John Colbeck**, is said to have been one of the first English settlers. Features which can still be seen include the slave dungeons adjoining the house.

SPANISH TOWN

Spanish Town, 14 miles (23km) west of Kingston on the A1 highway, appears at first to be an unprepossessing sprawl of modern low-rise concrete buildings. But Spanish Town is more than just a residential satellite of the capital. In 1523 its ideal location close to Kingston's natural harbour lured Spanish colonists away from their first settlement, which was unhealthily located near fever swamps at Sevilla la Nueva on the north coast. They called the new settlement Villa de la Vega (City of the Plain).

The Spaniards were not the first to see the advantages of what is now Spanish Town, for before they arrived this had been the site of the island's largest **Arawak** village. Nor were they the last – Cromwell's troops sacked the city in 1655 and built a new town on the ruins, which remained the seat of government until 1872. Relics of Spanish Town's heyday include the buildings around the square which rank among the region's finest surviving examples of 18th-century architecture. Built to show the wealth of the sugar industry, **Old Assembly House** (now the **Parish Council Building**) dominates the square's east side, with long brick arcades and wooden balconies. Like the **King's House**, on the opposite side of the square, it was built in 1762.

Rodney Memorial *

At the north end of the **Parade** – originally the central plaza of Villa de la Vega – stands the startlingly elegant Rodney Memorial, with its classic white marble colonnades and porticos. A toga-draped statue of **Admiral George Rodney**, a near-contemporary of Admiral Nelson, stands in front of the building, sheltered by a six-sided cupola. Rodney's fleet trounced a Spanish and French armada off Jamaica in 1782 .

Spanish Town Archaeological Museum *

The King's House, on the Parade, was built in 1762 and served as the town residence of the royal representative in Jamaica, the Governor, until the seat of government moved to Kingston. In 1925 it was partially destroyed in a fire, but its stylish Georgian portico and frontage have survived, while the reconstructed building within now houses a small collection of artefacts from the Spanish Town site, including Spanish doubloons, weapons and tools. Open 10:00–16:00 Monday–Friday.

Jamaican People's Museum of Craft and Technology *

Also on the Parade and situated alongside the King's House is the **Jamaican People's Museum of Craft and Technology**. This collection, housed in what was once the Governor's stables, includes exhibits of everyday tools, utensils and other bygones, including a recreation of a village store complete with stock. Open 10:00–16:00 Monday–Friday.

Cathedral of St Jago de la Vega *

Built in 1714, the cathedral stands on the Parade on the site of a 16th-century Spanish church of St Jago (St James) which was destroyed by the British invaders when they seized the town in 1655. With its carved wooden pews and interior columns, ceiling beams and colourful stained glass windows, it is considered by many as Jamaica's most beautiful church.

▲ *Above: Admiral Rodney's fleet kept Jamaica from French invasion during the 18th century.*
◄ *Opposite: Colbeck Castle was named after an early English settler who arrived in Jamaica with Oliver Cromwell's army in 1655.*

18TH-CENTURY WEALTH

By the mid-18th century there were more than 400 vast **sugar estates** on the island, each a self-sufficient entity. From his lavish, stone-built mansion, the planter (estate owner) was lord of all he surveyed, from the streets of slave barracks to the stables, the small houses of European clerks and overseers, the smoky buildings of the sugar mill and refining works, and the rolling green-gold sea of cane fields.

White Marl Taino Museum ★

This museum stands on the site of the island's largest Arawak village, 3 miles (5km) east of the town centre on the A1 highway. The village has been recreated with an exhibition of Arawak tools, weapons and utensils, and information on their long-lost way of life, reconstructed by archaeologists from the evidence found in the remnants of their settlement. Open 08:30–17:00 Mon–Thu, 08:30–16:00 Fri, closed Sat–Sun.

PORTMORE

Portmore's population has soared from around 80,000 to 150,000 since the 1980s. A 3-mile (5km) road causeway across **Kingston Harbour** connects the small residential town with the capital. South of the town lie the **Hellshire Hills**. This area of arid scrubland shelters a variety of rare species indigenous to Jamaica – including the Jamaican iguana and the rabbit-like Jamaican coney – but is gradually disappearing under a tide of new residential building. The southwest shore of the Hellshire peninsula is covered by muddy mangrove swamps which remain more attractive to the rare manatee than to the tourism industry. Nevertheless, the beaches of the east coast, close to Kingston, attract droves of city-dwellers every weekend. Portmore's other claim to fame is **Caymanas Park**, Jamaica's biggest racetrack. Racing takes place here every Wednesday and Saturday and on public holidays.

Hellshire Beaches ★★

On the east coast of the Hellshire peninsula, about three miles (5km) south of Portmore and across the bay from Kingston, a string of sandy beaches attract thousands of Kingstonians at weekends and on public holidays. For beach life Jamaican-style, head for **Fort Clarence Beach**, where there are frequent beauty shows, muscle contests, live music, beach games, barbecues, and food shacks selling fish, lobster and jerk meat. **Naggo Heads**, just north of Fort Clarence and separated from Portmore by the lagoon called the **Great Salt Pond**, is even more popular with local Jamaicans.

▼ *Below: The White Marl Museum contains a range of Arawak artefacts, some reconstructed on the basis of surviving evidence.*

BEST TIMES TO VISIT

Jamaica's climate is moderate year-round, but the heat and humidity May–November, along with seasonal rains, make it officially off-season.

GETTING THERE

A2 highway runs west from Negril through Savanna Mar and Black River into Middlesex, connecting Mandeville with May Pen and Spanish Town. The **A1 highway** connects Kingston with Spanish Town, Portmore, and the north coast.

GETTING AROUND

Off the highways, **roads** are poorly surfaced and erratically signposted. **Taxis** are best, but agree on a price in advance.

WHERE TO STAY

There are few hotels in Middlesex as most visitors just pass through. No recommended accommodation in Spanish Town, Portmore or May Pen.

Mandeville
MID-RANGE
Astra Country Inn, 62 Ward Avenue, Mandeville, tel: 962 3625, fax: 962 1461. 22 rooms, off-the-beach vacation. Good Jamaican restaurant.
Mandeville Hotel, 4 Hotel Street, Mandeville, tel: 962 2138, www.mandevillehotel jamaica.com 60 rooms; central, golf, tennis, coffee shop, pool, restaurants, bars.
Golf View Hotel, 51–2 Caledonia Avenue, Mandeville, tel: 962 4471/7, www.thegolf

viewhotel.com Modern, 45 room, overlooking golf course.

BUDGET
Kariba Kariba Guesthouse, 39 New Green Road, PO Box 482, Mandeville, Jamaica, tel: 962 3039, fax: 962 5502. Accessible; spacious rooms.

Milk River
MID-RANGE
Milk River Bath Hotel and Spa, Milk River, tel. 610 7745, milk riverhotel@yahoo.com Small, with an old-fashioned air (but a new pool) near the mineral pools. Meals on request.

Christiana
MID-RANGE
Hotel Villa Bella, Christiana, Manchester, tel: 964 2243, fax: 964 2765, www.hotelvilla bella.com Atmospheric, 18-room inn; excellent restaurant.

WHERE TO EAT

Mandeville has a selection of restaurants, but other options are in the few hotels, fast-food outlets and basic food shacks (Rasta fishermen at Farquhar's Beach, near Milk River, will cook fresh seafood with Jamaican trimmings).

Mandeville
LUXURY
Bloomfield Great House, 8 Perth Road, Mandeville, tel: 962 7130. Formerly the esteemed Bill Laurie's Steak House, and keeping up its traditions with great steaks, grills and Jamaican dishes.

MID-RANGE/BUDGET
Little Ochie, Alligator Pond, tel: 852 6430. This could be the best Jamaican food in the island, right on the beach and with rarely a tourist in sight. Worth a trip.

TOURS AND EXCURSIONS

Countryside Tours, based at the Astra Country Inn (*see* Where to Stay), has pioneered 'community-based tourism' with excursions throughout the region. Walking and riding in the Clarendon hills can also be arranged through the **Hotel Villa Bella** (*see* Where to Stay).
Kariba Leisure Tours, PO Box 482, Mandeville, tel: 962 8006, fax: 962 5502. Off-the-beaten-track excursions to Black River, Bamboo Avenue, Appleton Estate and the south coast.
Williamsfield Great House, tel: 963 4214. Tours by prior arrangement.
High Mountain Coffee Factory, tel: 963 4211. Tours by appointment only.
Pickapeppa Factory, tel: 962 2928. Tours of the factory and plantations by arrangement.
Marshall's Pen Great House, tel: 963 8569. Tours of house and grounds by arrangement.
Halse Hall, tel: 986 2215. Open to visitors by arrangement only.

USEFUL CONTACTS

Central and South Jamaica Tourism Committee, Astra Country Inn, 62 Ward Avenue, Mandeville, tel: 962 9758.

8
The Cayman Islands

The Cayman Islands could hardly present a greater contrast to Jamaica, less than an hour's flying time away. Jamaica is one of the Caribbean's biggest, most populous islands. Cayman (only visitors to this Caribbean microstate call it by its full name) comprises three tiny isles – the largest only 28 miles (44km) long and 7 miles (12km) wide. The archipelago has a population of only 30,000 multi-racial descendants of Cromwellian deserters, Spanish refugees, castaways and buccaneers who began settling the then uninhabited islands in around 1670, some 167 years after their discovery by **Christopher Columbus**. Cayman resorts are at once quieter, more relaxed and more up-market than Jamaica's upbeat beaches, and its people are much more reserved than their outgoing Caribbean neighbours.

The Cayman Islands has become one of the region's wealthier economies, thanks to extremely liberal banking and financial regulations that have attracted financiers and money manipulators from all over the world. This once sleepy nation of farmer-fishermen is now one of the world's most respected and sought-after financial centres. Cool sea breezes make the Cayman climate easier to deal with than the heat of the Jamaican coast, another bonus for its business visitors. Cayman's top attractions are both above and below the waterline – there are beaches to rival any in the Caribbean, an excellent golf course, island hideaways on the smaller isles and top-quality water sports, including diving.

DON'T MISS

*** Stingray City: snorkel with dozens of harmless, friendly giant rays.
*** Seven Mile Beach: powder white sand with great hotels and water sports.
** Mastic Trail: explore the Cayman wilderness.
** Turtle Farm: see hundreds of giant green turtles, hatched in captivity for release into the wild.
*** Scuba diving: hundreds of fantastic dive sites on all three islands.

◄ *Opposite: Boats anchor over Stingray City at Grand Cayman.*

113

THE CAYMAN ISLANDS

Underwater Cayman

It is below the surface that Cayman really shines, for this is one of the world's great diving destinations, with visibility of up to 200ft (60m) and abundant reef life for both shallow and deep divers. The three islands have too many perfect dive sites to list, with more than 150 shallow dives, wrecks and wall dives scattered around **Grand Cayman** alone. Grand Cayman is noted for its walls, some sloping gently, others plummeting into one of the world's deepest trenches. Wrecks off Grand Cayman include the *Doc Polson*, the *Oro Verde*, the *Balboa* and the LCM *David Nicholson*, all off the **West Side** of the island, and the *Ridgefield*, off the **East End**. Cayman Brac has the newest wreck in Cayman waters – the 330ft (100m) former Soviet warship *#356*. Cayman Brac also has wall dives and miles of shallow reefs, and **Bloody Bay Wall**, the best known of Little Cayman's dives, is a 1200ft (390m) vertical plunge which is rated one of the world's top dive sites. The latest addition to this ships' graveyard is the *USS Kittiwake*, scuttled off Seven Mile Beach in 2009.

GRAND CAYMAN

Grand Cayman is shaped like a whale swimming from west to east, with **Seven Mile Beach** running along the outer edge of its tail flipper and **George Town**, the island capital, at the base of the tail. **Rum Point**, midway along the north coast, forms the dorsal fin. The biggest and

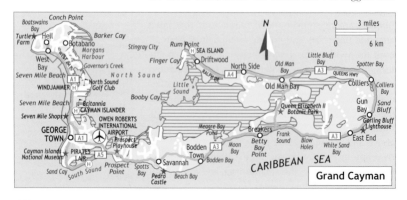

most populous of the three islands – with more than double the land area of the others – it is home to 26,000 islanders, some of them still fishermen and sailors, but many now involved in one of the two boom businesses which have put this tiny speck on the modern map of the Caribbean: banking and tourism. Its biggest beach is one of the finest in the Caribbean and thanks to a little ingenuity (including the invention of a special short-range golf ball), it has also become a golf destination.

George Town *

The Cayman capital, close to the south end of **Seven Mile Beach**, is mixture of old and new, with gleaming new international banks and duty-free shopping centres ousting older wooden buildings. Signs of the prosperity brought by tourism and international finance are everywhere, and the capital has a surprising choice of restaurants.

George Town is a duty-free port, with some outstanding shopping bargains. Also worth a visit is the **Cayman Islands National Museum** on Harbour Drive, which recreates a vanishing way of life, recording the days when Caymanians lived by seafaring. Open 09:00–17:00 Mon–Fri, and Sat 09:00–13:00 (www.museum.ky).

Britannia Golf Club ***

Created by Jack Nicklaus, the nine-hole Britannia Golf Club on West Bay Road, Seven Mile Beach – the island's first golf course and still the public course in the Caymans – is a challenging array of grassy knolls, sand dunes, lakes and yawning bunkers. In the early days of Cayman golf, players found that a ball hit too hard sank into the Caribbean, which almost surrounds the course (the tee shot from the fifth passes over a narrow stretch of ocean). The solution was the Cayman ball, which flies true, but has only half the range of a standard ball. Open daily, daylight hours (tel: 745 4653, www.britannia-golf.com).

▲ *Above: Prosperous George Town, the capital of the Cayman Islands, is the location of the National Museum.*

CAYMAN HISTORY

1503 Christopher Columbus sights the Caymans on his fourth voyage, naming them 'Las Tortugas' (the turtles) because of the huge numbers of green turtles in the surrounding waters.
1585 Sir Francis Drake's fleet anchors off Grand Cayman.
1668 Settlers from Jamaica are driven out of Little Cayman and Cayman Brac by Spanish pirates.
1670 Caymans become British by Treaty of Madrid.
1734 First settlers granted land in the Caymans.
1833 First permanent settlers move to Cayman Brac.

▲ *Above: Whether scuba diving or snorkelling, you are guaranteed colourful sights such as this giant anemone in the waters off the Cayman Islands.*

SAVING THE TURTLES

The **green turtles** which once filled Cayman waters in huge numbers were almost wiped out by excessive hunting over three centuries, but in 1971 the **Cayman Turtle Farm** was set up to study and hopefully boost the dwindling numbers. Thousands of eggs are rescued from Cayman beaches each year, and the hatchlings are raised in captivity for later release, increasing the percentage of hatchlings which survive to maturity. Around 30,000 farmed turtles have been tagged and released into the wild. Several thousand turtles each year are also raised for their meat, which is popular with Caymanians but cannot be exported.

Seven Mile Beach ★★★

This must be one of the world's finest beaches. Running from just north of **George Town** to **North West Point**, Seven Mile Beach has powder white sand, transparent waters, and water sports including world-class diving, windsurfing, parasailing, jet skiing, dinghy sailing and snorkelling among its many attractions.

North Sound Golf Club ★★★

This 18-hole, par 71 course, on SafeHaven Drive, has established the Cayman Islands as a world-class golfing destination, and attracts a number of golfing enthusiasts to its impressive facilities. Open daily, daylight hours (tel: 947 4653, www.northsoundclub.com).

Stingray City ★★★

In only 12ft (4m) of clear water in the **North Sound**, this must surely be the best of the world's shallow-water dive sites, accessible to both snorkellers and complete novices as well as experienced scuba divers. Dozens of stingrays lurk on the bottom of the North Sound. Gentle and harmless, these creatures are accustomed to being fed by divers and will take titbits of squid or fish from your fingers.

Queen Elizabeth II Botanic Park ★

Opened by Queen Elizabeth II in 1994, this award-winning 60-acre (24ha) park on Frank Sound Road was established to conserve more than 200 endangered trees and plants, from ironwood and thatch palm to superb orchids – go in May or June to see the best display – as well as birds, including the Grand Cayman parrot and the West Indian woodpecker, and reptiles such as the Grand Cayman blue iguana and the blue-throated Cayman anole lizard. Open daily Oct–Mar 09:00–17:30, Apr–Sep 09:00–18:30 (www.botanic-park.ky). Also within the Botanic Park is the outstanding **Mastic Trail**. Plunge into the bush on a guided tour of the last remaining Grand Cayman wilderness, with the chance to see rare parrots, ajouti, land crabs, iguanas and hundreds of rare flowers, shrubs and trees. Guided tours are conducted at 08:30 daily.

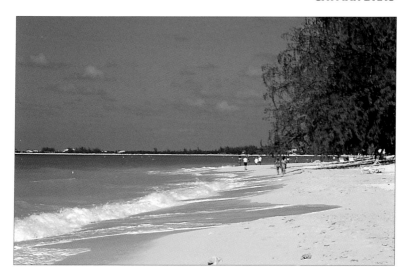

Botswain's Beach and Cayman Islands Turtle Farm *

The government-owned turtle farm hopes to save the endangered green turtles of the Caribbean by hatching thousands of eggs laid on Cayman's beaches each year and releasing hatchling turtles into the sea. Botswains Beach also has swimming and snorkelling lagoons, touch tanks full of rays and dogfish, and an open-air shark pool. Open 08:00–16:30 Mon–Sat (825 North West Point Rd, West Bay, tel. 949 3834, www.botswainsbeach.ky).

CAYMAN BRAC

Compared with low-lying Grand Cayman, the Brac, 90 miles (145km) to the west, is truly mountainous. The island is some 12 miles (20km) long and no more than one mile (1.8km) wide. The ridge which forms its backbone soars to 140ft (42m) above sea level and is riddled with caves which are said to have been used to hide pirates and their treasure. Many of the islanders are employed in the fishing industry or as merchant seamen, making their homes in **Stake Bay**, the village on the north coast which is the nearest thing Cayman Brac has to a capital.

▲ *Above: Heavenly Seven Mile Beach runs almost the length of the west end of Grand Cayman.*

BLACK CORAL

You will see stores advertising black coral jewellery in **George Town** and other parts of **Grand Cayman**. Found at many depths, the best black coral is found below the 100ft (30m) level and grows slowly – about ⅓ inch (7mm) a year. In 1978, the Islands banned the removal of live black coral from Cayman reefs, but it is now imported from **Belize** and **Honduras**. This smacks of hypocrisy and you are advised not to buy any.

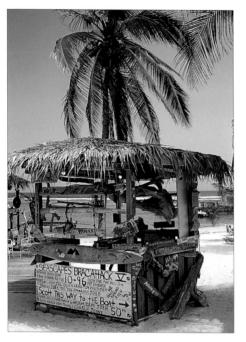

Cut off from the world until the 1960s, 'the Brac' now has an airport which can handle international jets and daily flights from Miami, its own schools and hospital. Young men increasingly head for the bright lights of Grand Cayman or Miami instead of working at sea, and beachfront building lots sell for $50 per square metre or more. That said, Cayman Brac remains a pious and conservative society, with no fewer than 14 churches scattered around the island for a population of 1400 people. Almost all settlement is around the coast, while the interior of the island is a mass of low tropical scrub growing from jagged limestone rock.

▲ *Above: Although Cayman Brac's shoreline is predominantly rocky, there is a small sandy beach in the southwest of the island.*

Russian Destroyer ★★

Purchased from the Russian Navy as scrap and deliberately sunk off the West End as a dive attraction, this wreck is the only diveable Soviet warship in Western waters. The ship was scuttled in 10–60ft (3–20m) of water in September 1996, and the wreck, colonised by marine flora and fauna, offers great diving.

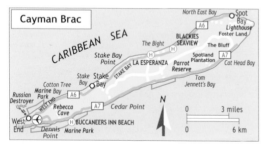

The Bluff ★★

There are fantastic views from this jungle-covered 140ft (45m) cliff at the island's north end, which is crowned by a small lighthouse. A continuous line of limestone cliffs sweeps away in either direction.

LITTLE CAYMAN

Little Cayman is the next best thing to a private island. About 5 miles (8km) west of Cayman Brac, part of the island's interior is a nature reserve, protecting a host of rare birds – including red-footed boobies, frigate birds, and West Indian whistling ducks – and reptiles such as the wild iguana, as well as plants, including orchids.

Bloody Bay Marine Park ★★★

The park boasts some amazing dive sites ranging from shallow dives on a fantastic coral reef to deep dives on one of the world's finest vertical walls. There are 22 dives in all, with **Great Wall West** rated as the one not to miss. Fish include eagle ray, various groupers, garden eels, plus turtles, brightly coloured sponges, and corals in excellent condition. The marine park is 25 minutes from the handful of resorts on Little Cayman.

Booby Reserve and National Trust House ★★

Flocks of gannet-like boobies and their aerial adversaries, frigate birds, both nest around the shores of this inland mangrove lagoon and can be viewed from the verandah of the pretty wooden National Trust House, which houses a small exhibition on Cayman Brac's environment. Open 09:00–12:00, 15:00–16:30 weekdays.

Tarpon Lake ★★

The giant tarpon, up to 6ft (2m) long and armoured in silver scales up to 1½ inches (3cm) in diameter, is one of the most prized game fishes in the Caribbean. Tarpon are usually marine fish, but a breeding population were trapped in this brackish lagoon, 7½ miles (12km) west of the airstrip, centuries ago when it was cut off from the sea. A wooden walkway leads from the roadside out into the waters of the lagoon.

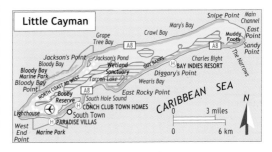

BEST TIMES TO VISIT

Visit year-round, but Jul–Sep is very hot and damp.

Air Jamaica and **Cayman**

GETTING THERE

Airways offer flights between Grand Cayman and Kingston (1hr). Cayman Airways' jets connect Grand Cayman with Miami (90 mins) and Cayman Brac (17 mins). **Island Air** flies Twin Otters between Grand Cayman, Cayman Brac and Little Cayman (45 mins).

GETTING AROUND

By road: Car rental companies include **Avis**, tel: 949 2468, www.aviscayman.com **Thrifty**, tel: 949 6640; **Eurocar**, tel: 947 3681; and others (full list available at www.cayman islands.co.uk/transportation). Motor scooters can be hired on Grand Cayman from **Scooters and Wheels**, tel: 949 0064, www.scooters@cay-man.com and on Little Cayman from **Scooters!**, tel: 916 4971. On Grand Cayman, bicycles can be rented from **Cayman Cycle Rentals**, tel: 945 4021. Taxis are readily available, but there are few bus services.

By sea: Ferries from Hyatt Dock to Rum Point and Cayman Kai.

George Town

WHERE TO STAY

LUXURY

Coconut Harbour, PO Box 2086, George Town, tel: 949 7468. Comfortable, waterfront hotel; diving on Waldo's Reef.

MID-RANGE

Sunset House, PO Box 479, George Town, tel: 949 7111, www.sunsethouse.com Run by divers; outskirts of town.

BUDGET

Eldemire's Tropical Inn, 18 Pebbles Way, George Town, tel: 916 8369, www.eldemire. com This family-run guest-house with pool, a short walk from George Town and the beach, offers perhaps the best value on the island.

Shangri-La Bed and Breakfast, Seven Mile Beach, tel: 526 1170, www.shangri labandb.com Luxurious six-bedroom guesthouse, five minutes from the sands of Seven Mile Beach.

Tropical Breeze at Breakers, 1169 Bodden Town Road, tel: 916 0318, www.caymans seasidevillas.com Oceanfront cottages with views of Seven Mile beach, twelve miles from George Town.

Seven Mile Beach

LUXURY

Caribbean Club, PO Box 11, Seven Mile Beach, tel: 623 4500, www.caribclub.com Central, no children under 11 in winter.

Ritz Carlton Grand Cayman, Seven Mile Beach, tel: 943 9000, www.ritzcarlton.com Grandest and most luxurious hotel on the island, with 365 rooms and suites and facilities including five restaurants, tennis centre and private nine-hole golf course.

Westin Casuarina Resort,

Box 30620, tel: 945 3800, www. westingrandcayman.com Luxury resort on the best stretch of Seven Mile Beach.

MID-RANGE

Christopher Columbus Condos, 2013 West Bay Road, tel: 945 4354, www. christophercolumbuscondos. com Two- and three-bedroom self-catering apartments on the beach with facilities including floodlit tennis courts, maid service, laundry and concierge.

Lighthouse Point, 571 Northwest Point Road, tel: 946 5658, www.lighthouse. point-cayman.com Unique eco-resort with nine ocean-front condo apartments built using green technologies such as solar and windpower, with facilities including bistro and award-winning dive centre.

BUDGET

Turtle Nest Inn, 166 Bodden Town Road, Bodden Town, tel: 947 8665, www.turtlenest inn.com Eight stylish self-catering apartments with pool.

Cayman Brac

MID-RANGE

La Esperanza, Box 28, Stake Bay, Cayman Brac, tel: 948 0531, www.laesperanza.net Five comfortable condos.

BUDGET

Walton's Mango Manor, Stake Bay, tel/fax: 948 0518, www. waltonsmangomanor.com Up-market; five air-con rooms.

Little Cayman

LUXURY

Conch Club Town Homes, PO Box 51, Blossom Village, Little Cayman, tel: 948 1033, www.conchclubcondos.com Condominiums.

Pirates Point Resort, Preston Bay, Little Cayman, tel: 948 1010, www.piratespoint resort.com 10-room all-inclusive resort; offers diving and a dive shop.

MID-RANGE

Paradise Villas, PO Box 30, tel: 948 0001, fax: 948 0002, www.paradisevillas.com 12 air-conditioned, one-bedroom condominiums.

BUDGET

Little Cayman Cottage, PO Box 35, Blossom Village, tel/fax: 948 0095. Intimate cottage, good value for money.

WHERE TO EAT

George Town

LUXURY

Casanova by the Sea, 65 North Church Street, tel: 949 7633. A good Italian seafood restaurant located on the George Town waterfront. Has ocean views and an excellent wine list.

Lobster Pot, 245 North Church Street, tel: 949 2736. This is the oldest restaurant on the island and is famed for its seafood, such as sesame-seared yellowfin tuna, red snapper with sautéed bananas, conch, and more.

MID-RANGE

Rockfish Lounge, Tropical Plaza, Smith Road, tel: 943 8600. Restaurant and bar with a strong local and Caribbean flavour and menu which includes West Indian curry shrimp, Cayman style snapper, and sirloin steaks.

BUDGET

The Brasserie Market, Cricket Square, Elgin Avenue, tel: 945 1814. Salads, sand-wiches and full meals in this breezy café-bar which takes pride in using fresh, locally sourced ingredients.

Seven Mile Beach/West Bay

LUXURY

Cracked Conch, North West Point, West Bay tel: 945 5217. Waterfront location, famed for its Sunday brunches and Caribbean fusion menu which includes the eponymous cracked conch, conch chowder, conch fritters … as well as dishes such as seared snapper and roast lobster.

MID-RANGE

Ray Ray's, 426 West Bay Road, Seven Mile Beach; no tel. This is the best place in Grand Cayman to sample Caribbean-style jerk pork and chicken, barbecued ribs and beef, Ray Ray's is a late-night fixture (opening around 22:00–04:00, Thursday and Friday only).

BUDGET

Azzurro Café, Buckingham Square, tel: 946 7745. Pasta, patisserie, salads and sand-wiches make this one of the best budget options on Seven Mile Beach.

TOURS AND EXCURSIONS

Rudy's Travellers Transport, PO Box 310, West Bay, Grand Cayman, tel: 949 3208, fax: 949 1155.

Vernon's Sightseeing Tours, PO Box 312, West Bay, Grand Cayman, tel: 949 1509, fax: 949 0213.

Seaborne Flightseeing Adventures, PO Box 2433, Grand Cayman, tel: 949 6029, fax: 949 7044.

Cayman Islands Department

USEFUL CONTACTS

of Tourism, The Pavilion, Cricket Square, PO Box 67, George Town, Grand Cayman, tel: 949 0623, www.caymanislands.co.uk

CAYMAN ISLES	J	F	M	A	M	J	J	A	S	O	N	D
AVERAGE TEMP. °C	29	29	29	31	31	32	32	32	32	30	27	29
AVERAGE TEMP. °F	84	84	84	88	88	90	90	90	90	86	81	84
RAINFALL mm	25	25	25	75	100	75	100	150	150	200	50	25
RAINFALL ins.	1	1	1	3	4	3	4	6	6	8	2	1
DAYS OF RAINFALL	1	1	1	3	4	3	4	6	6	6	2	1

Travel Tips

Tourist Information
JAMAICA
Jamaica Tourist Board offices:
UK: 1–2 Prince Consort Rd, London SW7 2BZ, tel: 0207 225 9090, fax: 0207 224 0551, web: www.visitjamaica.com
USA: 1500 N Michigan Ave no. 1030, Chicago, IL 60611, tel: 312 527 1296, fax: 312 627 1472; 1320 South Dixie Highway, Suite 1101, Coral Gables, Miami, FL 33146, toll free: 1 800 233 4JTB, tel: 1 305 665 0557, fax: 1 305 666 7239, email: jamaicatrvl@aol.com; 301 2nd Avenue, New York, NY 10017, tel: 212 866 9727 or 800 233 4582, fax: 212 866 9730; 3440 Wilshire Blvd no. 1207, LA, CA 90010, tel: 213 384 1123, fax: 213 384 1780.
Canada: 303 Eglinton Ave East, Suite 202, Toronto, toll free: 1 800 465 2624, tel: 1 416 482 7850, fax: 1 416 482 1730, email: jtb@jtbcanada.com
Head Office: 64 Knutsford Boulevard, Kingston 5, Jamaica, tel: 1 876 929 9200/19, fax: 1 876 929 9375, web: www.visitjamaica.com

CAYMAN ISLANDS
Cayman Islands Department of Tourism (CIDoT): London, LA, Chicago, Houston, Miami, NY and Toronto. **Head Office:** CIDoT, The Pavilion, Cricket Square, PO Box 67, George Town, Grand Cayman, tel: 345 949 0623, fax: 345 949 4053, www.caymanislands.co.uk

Entry Requirements
JAMAICA and CAYMAN
No visa required for British, US, Australian, Canadian, and other British Commonwealth or European Union citizens. South African nationals require visas.

Customs
JAMAICA
Duty-free import allowances: 25 cigars, 200 cigarettes, 1 pint (550ml) of liquor, 1 pound of tobacco and 1 quart (1 litre) of wine. Importing rum, coffee and marijuana is forbidden.

CAYMAN ISLANDS
Duty-free import allowances: 1 quart (1 litre) of spirits, 2 bottles of wine, up to 200 cigarettes or equivalent in cigars or tobacco.

Health Requirements
JAMAICA
No special vaccination requirements, but you may want to consider immunisation against tetanus, diphtheria, typhoid and hepatitis. Dengue fever (carried by mosquitoes) is present in some locations off the beaten track – no prophylaxis is available for dengue so avoid being bitten.

CAYMAN ISLANDS
No special health precautions.

Getting There
By Air JAMAICA: Air Jamaica is the major carrier to Jamaica (Kingston and Montego Bay) from the UK (London Heathrow), with three-tier service and a new de luxe economy section which offers some extra comfort at affordable fares. Air Jamaica also flies from numerous points in the USA and Canada, and from Germany. Other carriers from the UK include British Airways and Virgin Atlantic.
By Air CAYMAN ISLANDS: Air Jamaica and Cayman Airways fly between Kingston and Grand Cayman. Cayman

Airways and numerous other US carriers fly between Grand Cayman and Miami and major US and Canadian airports.

By Sea: Cruise ships from Miami call at Mo Bay, Kingston, Ocho Rios and Port Antonio in **Jamaica** and at George Town in **Cayman**. There are no regular inter-island **ferries**.

What to Pack
JAMAICA
Beachwear, long-sleeved shirts, a hat, sunscreen and mosquito repellant are essential (all are expensive in Jamaica). Evening-wear ranges from casual (shorts and T-shirt) to jacket and tie at posh restaurants.

CAYMAN ISLANDS
See Jamaica *above*. You can rent snorkelling and scuba equipment on all three islands.

Money Matters
JAMAICA
Currency: Jamaican dollar notes in denominations of J$1, J$2, J$10, J$20, J$50, J$100, and coins for J$5, J$1, and 50, 25, 20 and 10 cents. Most services are in US dollars, which are widely accepted. US-dollar travellers' cheques are prefer-able to other currencies. Credit cards are widely accepted.
Exchange: Money can be exchanged at banks in major towns, most hotels and licensed exchange bureaux.

CAYMAN ISLANDS
Currency: Cayman dollar. Most accommodation is priced in US dollars, which

are acceptable everywhere as an alternative to local currency. Changing sterling or US dollars into local currency is usually not much of a prob-lem, and major credit cards are accepted by almost all hotels, restaurants, car and bike rental agencies, tour and scuba companies.
Tipping: A 10% tip is normal in most hotels or restaurants. However, some restaurants add a service charge to the bill, in which case there is no need to tip any further. A few all-inclusive resorts follow a no-tipping policy.

Accommodation
JAMAICA
Jamaica has accommodation to suit all holiday budgets, ranging from luxury villas with your own household staff to cheap and cheerful guesthouses and self-catering bungalows and apartments. The most luxurious villas are concentrated around **Port Antonio**, and close to the Hanover coast, west of Montego Bay. **Montego Bay** and **Ocho Rios** have an excellent choice of guesthouse accommodation and mid-to-budget range hotels. **Negril** has by far the biggest choice of simple budget guesthouses and apartments, and even cheaper accommodation can be found around Bluefields and Treasure Beach, on the Westmoreland and St Elizabeth coasts.
Kingston has a narrower choice of accommodation for visitors, most of it in the mid-range to upper price brackets and designed mainly with the business traveller in mind.

Jamaica pioneered the concept of the **all-inclusive resort,** which has now caught on throughout the Caribbean. At luxury resorts such as those in the Sandals, Couples, and Grand Lido groups and at a number of independently owned imitators, everything from accommodation to unlimited food, drink, land and water sports is included in one fixed package price. There are varying degrees of luxury (e.g. some resorts offer only Jamaican alcoholic beverages, while others include imported wines, beers and spirits) and the all-inclusives can offer excellent value for your money. Some of these unique resorts are reserved exclusively for couples, while others cater to families and some are rather notorious for fun-loving singles. These all-inclusive resorts can be found around Montego Bay,

Ocho Rios and Negril. Island Resorts, owned by the Jamaican music industry entrepreneur Chris Blackwell, has some superbly characterful hotels in out of the way places, such as Strawberry Hill in the Blue Mountains and Jake's at Treasure Beach. Jamaica also offers around 40 small **inn-style hotels**, many of them in idyllic locations away from the razzmatazz of the big resorts, grouped under the title 'Inns of Jamaica'. For information on these and all other types of accommodation, contact the Jamaica Tourist Board.

CAYMAN ISLANDS

Grand Cayman has more than 60 places to stay, almost all of them along **Seven Mile Beach**, with a handful elsewhere. Accommodation ranges from budget guesthouses for scuba divers to luxury hotels for the well-heeled traveller, but the accent is definitely on the more **expensive** end of the price scale. Self-catering condominium apartments are substantially cheaper than luxury hotels, and offer a value-for-money compromise, especially for families, with luxury accommodation, landscaped grounds and swimming pools, and fully equipped kitchens which mean you can save money on food and drink.

Eating Out

JAMAICA

Whether you savour grilled lobster, prawns or red snapper on the beach at Negril, barbecued pork or chicken at a downtown Kingston jerk centre, mouth-watering mangoes with a dash of lime or pineapple dusted with cayenne pepper, Jamaica is at its best when offering deliciously fresh, simply prepared local produce. The island is almost equally good at franchised international fast food, and you'll find no shortage of burgers, pizzas, pasta or fried chicken. Most mid-range hotels and all-inclusive resorts offer buffet meals, with a choice of international and local cuisine such as rice and peas or ackee and saltfish. Kingston has its share of sophisticated restaurants, some of them fostering a new Jamaican style of cooking that makes the most of home-grown produce. Elsewhere, many restaurants tend to place too much emphasis on stylish trappings and not enough on the food, which can be bland and overpriced. All wine is imported, and indifferent wines may be wildly overpriced in more pretentious restaurants.

CAYMAN ISLANDS

Fresh fish and seafood are top of the menu, but Cayman offers everything from local dishes to French, British, Italian, Chinese, American and Mexican cuisine, with most of the restaurants on Grand Cayman close to Seven Mile Beach. Local specialities include the conch, an enormous shellfish – which appears in stews, fritters, marinades and chowder – and breadfruit, which is served boiled, fried, roasted or baked. On Cayman Brac and Little Cayman, almost all restaurants are attached to hotels and guesthouses, and the menu tends to be simpler and a little more limited, but no less well prepared.

Transport

JAMAICA

Air: Air Jamaica's internal services connect Kingston with Montego Bay (**Air Jamaica**, tel: 876 923 8680 or 924 8850, www.air jamaica.com). Air taxis also connect Kingston's Tinson Pen Airport with Montego Bay, Negril, Boscobel (Ocho Rios) and Port Antonio.

CONVERSION CHART

FROM	TO	MULTIPLY BY
Millimetres	Inches	0.0394
Metres	Yards	1.0936
Metres	Feet	3.281
Kilometres	Miles	0.6214
Square kilometres	Square miles	0.386
Hectares	Acres	2.471
Litres	Pints	1.760
Kilograms	Pounds	2.205
Tonnes	Tons	0.984

To convert Celsius to Fahrenheit: x 9 ÷ 5 + 32

TRAVEL TIPS

These include Tim Air (www.timair.net) which is based in Montego Bay.
Road: To rent a car, you will need a valid drivers licence from your country of residence. Roads are generally poor and accidents not uncommon, so you should have comprehensive insurance cover. Drivers must be at least 25 years old and must post a bond (using cash, credit card, or travellers' cheques) to meet insurance requirements. Service stations are open daily and will only accept cash. Speed limit is 30mph (48kph) in built-up areas, 50mph (80kph) on highways. Drive on the left.
Road maps area available from the JTB and from the **Jamaican Union of Travellers Association**, 8 Claude Clarke Avenue, PO Box 1155, Montego Bay 1, tel: 876 968 7088, fax: 876 974 9142. Driving at night is not recommended.
Bus: Public transport is inadequate, with chaotic schedules, hopelessly overcrowded and poorly maintained vehicles and a good chance of losing at least some of your possessions. Forget it.
Train: The public transport service on the rather rickety railway line which runs between Kingston and Montego Bay – a spectacular ride – has unfortunately been suspended.

CAYMAN ISLANDS
Air: Cayman Airways connects Grand Cayman

with Cayman Brac and Little Cayman.
Road: Driving is on the left of the road. Full driving licence and insurance are required for rentals. Observe the signs for one-way streets in George Town and do not pass stationary buses, as the doors open into the middle of the road (the buses are imported from the USA and are designed for driving on the right). Full insurance and collision damage waiver is recommended. Maps are available from the **Cayman Islands Department of Tourism**. There is no motorists' association.

Trading Hours
JAMAICA
Banks are open 09:00–14:00 Mon–Thu, 09:00–15:00 Fri, with some also open Friday afternoon 14:30–17:00.
Offices are usually open 09:00–17:00 Mon–Fri and **shops** open 08:30–17:00 Mon–Sat, with a half day on Wednesday.

CAYMAN ISLANDS
Banks are open 09:00–13:00, 14:00–16:00 Mon–Fri.
Government offices are open 09:00–17:00 Mon–Fri.
Shops are mostly open 08:30–12:00 and 14:00–17:00, as well as half day Saturday, and are closed Sunday, but many of the duty-free shops may have longer shopping hours.

Time
Both **Jamaica** and the **Cayman Islands** are on GMT –5 year-round.

Communications
JAMAICA
The external dialling code for all Jamaican telephone numbers is **876**. All the up-market hotels have direct dial. Telephone service in theory operates 24hr a day but the system is overstretched and it can be difficult to get a connection at peak times. Operator assistance: tel: **112** (local) or **113** (international). There are no 24hr post offices in Jamaica. Fax facilities are available in almost all the hotels and guesthouses.

CAYMAN ISLANDS
For international calls to the Cayman Islands dial the code **00 345**). All Grand Cayman, Cayman Brac and Little Cayman telephone and fax numbers share the same first two digits (**94**), which are omitted for local calls. Telephone service operates 24hr a day. No 24hr post offices. Fax facilities available from all major hotels.

Electricity
Jamaica and the **Caymans** use US current and electrical fittings, 110/115 volt, 60-cycle current.

HOLIDAYS AND FESTIVALS

JAMAICA
New Year's Day • Ash Wednesday • Good Friday • Easter Monday • Labour Day (23 May) • Independence Day (first Monday in Aug) • National Heroes' Day (third Mon in Oct) • Christmas Day • Boxing Day.
Festivals:
Reggae SunSplash (usually in Aug)

CAYMAN ISLANDS
New Year's Day • Ash Wednesday • Good Friday • Easter Monday • Discovery Day (19 May) • the Queen's Birthday • Constitution Day (7 July) • Remembrance Day (November) • Christmas Day and Boxing Day.
Festivals:
Easter Regatta • Million Dollar Month Fishing Tournament (June) • Cayman Islands International Aviation Week (June/July) • Pirates Week Festival (October)

Weights and Measures
Jamaica and the **Cayman Islands** officially use old-fashioned British Imperial weights and measures (pounds and ounces for weight, pints and gallons for liquids) but as almost everything is imported from the USA, most quantities are in US pounds, ounces and fluid measures (fluid ounces, pints, quarts and gallons). Distances are metric.

Health Precautions
No special health precautions are required by law for either of the destinations. The tap water is safe to drink in both **Jamaica** and the **Cayman Islands**. Visitors from cooler climes should beware of sunburn and heat exhaustion (especially in the Cayman Islands, where shade can be in short supply); be sure to use adequate sunscreen and drink plenty of fluids.
Malaria is not endemic, but in late 2006 there was an outbreak of the disease in the Kingston area, with more than 150 cases reported. Visitors may wish to check UK Foreign Office or US State Department health advice before visiting Kingston. To be safe, some visitors may choose to have themselves and their family vaccinated against tetanus, diphtheria, typhoid and hepatitis, although these precautions are seldom essential.
See also Health Requirements on p. 122.

Health Services
Good, modern health services in clinics and hospitals are available in both **Jamaica** and the **Cayman Islands**, but adequate medical insurance cover is essential as medical services in this region are extremely costly.

Security
JAMAICA
Jamaica has an extremely high rate of violent crime (as many as 1500 murders a year) and tourists, especially those who dabble in drug purchases, are far from immune. Walking any distance after dark is not advised, and ghetto areas of urban Kingston should be avoided at all times. Incidents may be reported to local police stations.

CAYMAN ISLANDS
Cayman is one of the safest places in the world, with very little violent crime and only a small amount of petty pilfering. Valuables should be kept in hotel safes or safe deposits.

Emergencies
JAMAICA
Police: dial **911**
Fire and ambulance: dial **110**

CAYMAN ISLANDS
All emergencies: dial **911**

GOOD READING

Frank Bernal *Birds of Jamaica* (Heinemann Caribbean, 1989). Definitive guide to Jamaican bird life.
Colin Channer *Iron Balloons: Hit Fiction* (Akashic Boooks, 2006).
Jean Rhys *Wide Sargasso Sea;* (Palgrave Macmillan, 2003).
Ian Thomson *The Dead Yard: Tales of Modern Jamaica* (Faber & Faber, 2009).
David Katz *olid Foundation: An Oral History of Reggae* (Bloomsbury, 2003).